The Essential Guide to Optical Networks

ISBN 0-13-042956-2

90000

9 780130 429568

Prentice Hall PTR
Essential Guide Series

THE ESSENTIAL GUIDE TO APPLICATION SERVICE PROVIDERS

Toigo

THE ESSENTIAL GUIDE TO STORAGE AREA NETWORKS

Vacca

THE ESSENTIAL GUIDE TO MOBILE BUSINESS

Vos & deKlein

THE ESSENTIAL GUIDE TO COMPUTING: THE STORY OF INFORMATION TECHNOLOGY

Walters

THE ESSENTIAL GUIDE TO RF AND WIRELESS

Weisman

The
Essential
Guide to
Optical Networks

DAVID GREENFIELD

Prentice Hall PTR, Upper Saddle River, NJ 07458
www.phptr.com

A Cataloging-in-Publication Data record for this book can be obtained from the Library of Congress.

Editorial/Production supervisor: *Faye Gemmellaro*
Acquisitions editor: *Mary Franz*
Editorial assistant: *Noreen Regina*
Cover designer: *Bruce Kenselaar*
Cover design director: *Jerry Votta*
Art director: *Gail Cocker-Bogusz*
Interior series design: *Meg VanArsdale*
Manufacturing manager: *Maura Zaldivar*
Marketing manager: *Dan DePasquale*

 © 2002 Prentice Hall PTR
Prentice-Hall, Inc.
Upper Saddle River, NJ 07458

Prentice Hall books are widely used by corporations and government
agencies for training, marketing, and resale.

The publisher offers discounts on this book when ordered in bulk
quantities. For more information, contact:

Corporate Sales Department
Phone: 800-382-3419
Fax: 201-236-7141
Email: corpsales@prenhall.com

Or write:

Prentice Hall PTR
Corp. Sales Dept.
One Lake Street
Upper Saddle River, NJ 07458

Printed in the United States of America
10   9   8   7   6   5   4   3   2   1

ISBN: 0-13-042956-2

Pearson Education LTD.
Pearson Education Australia PTY, Limited
Pearson Education Singapore, Pte. Ltd.
Pearson Education North Asia Ltd.
Pearson Education Canada, Ltd.
Pearson Educación de Mexico, S.A. de C.V.
Pearson Education—Japan
Pearson Education Malaysia, Pte. Ltd.

Contents

Preface

Welcome! If you've come this far, you must have an interest in the fascinating world of optical networking. It's a world that stands to revolutionize computer networks and the people who use them—you and I.

Despite the huge implications and the captivating technology involved in optical networks, surprisingly little has been written for the nontechnical audience. Engineers and like-minded folk will find numerous books out there, with all the right formulas and equations to make a normal man's eyes bulge, but for those of us who think in words and not square roots, optical networking remains a largely opaque field. Some noise gets through about terabits of capacity, historic changes, and the like, but darned little is intelligible to the reader outside of the optical club.

Hence this book. In its pages we'll explore the fascinating worlds of lasers, switches, and optical networks. We'll cover the basics of fibers and the components needed to connect them. We'll get a close-up look at the best-known optical technology—wave-division multiplexing—and how it works.

But today's optical networks aren't just about fibers strung together. All sorts of new technologies are making it easier for businesses and consumers to jump on a light-speed connection at a more affordable price. Other technologies are changing the very way carriers build the heart or core of the networks. Some are even enabling optics to alter their very characteristics, depending on the types of data.

These technologies aren't normally considered optical, yet they are critical to understanding how optical networks—or, more specifically, the public optical network—is evolving. We'll cover these technologies without the gadzillions of numbers or mind-boggling equations normally used to explain this optical stuff.

Of course, there's a tradeoff. The information here won't enable you to go out and build an optical network. If that's your goal, you'll find a bunch of other books out there that can help. But if you're in marketing or sales, law, research, human resources, or project management—if you're a student, an engineer looking to switch areas, or anyone looking for an overview, refresher, or just a plain easy read—you've come to the right place.

To those ends, *The Essential Guide to Optical Networks* is designed to be accessible on multiple levels. The text of the book should be understandable to those with a non-mathematical or scientific background. Those who crave formulas will get them in our "Dr. Geek" sidebars spread throughout the book. You'll also find key words bolded in the text; these are later defined in the glossary for easy reference. Cartoons appearing in each chapter present the lighter side of optical networking (yes, there is such a thing).

Those without any knowledge of the industry would do well to start out with Part I, Chapter 1; it provides an overview and explains where we're going. Chapter 2 is meant for those of us who might have had a little exposure to the world of networking or might be familiar with voice networks, but have less knowledge of data networks. We'll walk through the various technologies that are needed to build corporate networks and that increasingly are being used for building the new public network.

Part II is aimed at those looking to understand the bread-and-butter of optical networks—the fibers and components. Chapter 3 explains the relevant physics involved in sending a signal down an optical fiber. In Chapter 4, we'll look at the types of fibers used and the challenges in sending signals down those fibers. Chapter 5 explains the different kinds of components for building out fiber networks from amplifiers to lasers, filters to couplers. Then we wrap up in Chapter 6 with a look at the different kinds of switches used to build the public network.

Part III moves beyond the traditional optical technologies to look at the emerging access and signaling technologies needed to build tomorrow's network. Chapter 7 gives a refresher on SONET, the standard for building out public networks today. Chapter 8 looks at the emerging techniques for replacing SONET in the core of the network. Chapter 9 looks at the technologies vying to replace SONET in the access to customer premises. Finally, Chapter 10 looks at technologies being used to bind the services and the infrastructure together.

It's a fascinating world. I hope you enjoy reading about it as much as I've enjoyed writing about it.

Acknowledgments

Obviously a project like this book depends on the help of many people. Engineers and Ph.D.s, friends and colleagues from around the globe provided valuable assistance.

Hoping not to miss anyone, I want to extend my gratitude to these generous folk. One thing that's important in writing a book like this is getting inside the mind of an operator, and toward this end numerous people provided valuable assistance. Williams Communications' Scott Beudoin and Scott Pohlman as well as Savvis Communications' Rick Bubenik, Greg Graff, Jason Gutenschwager, and Mike Gordon were gracious with their time. Ebone's Sean Doran, John Shearing, and Leo McCloskey provided a more European perspective. A special thanks goes, of course, to Ebone's Pedro Falcao for penning his unique views on the evolution of WDM.

Part II looks at the fiber and components that underlie the intelligent optical network, and 3M's Barbara Birrell provided valuable input here. Corning's Steve Swanson was a huge help in this area and in particular in putting together what eventually became Appendix A of this book. A big thanks to author Jeff Hecht who graciously allowed us to use many of the formulas he accumulated in his book, *Understanding Fiber Optics*, one of the best written texts in the area. Michael Factor's detailed and conscientious work on optical components made the chapter on this topic possible and kept this journalist on the straight and narrow. In the fascinating area of optical switches Sycamore's Naimish Patel was a huge help. His comments significantly improved the chapter on this topic.

Part III is largely a study of emerging technologies. These areas are moving targets and a number of people helped freeze the picture, if only for a moment. Savvis' Greg Graff helped me greatly in fine-tuning my knowledge of the world of SONET. Sprint's Mark Jones took the time to read and comment on much of the SONET manuscript, offering invaluable comments along the way. Lucent's Enrique Hernandez-Valencia, author of the generic framing procedure (GFP), provided information about the protocol that bears his mark.

Plenty of new technologies are hoping to challeng SONET in the metro. RPR is often talked about as a favorite. A big thanks to Mindspeed's Lauren Schlicht, Nortel's John Hawkins, and Cisco's Mike Takefman for helping to rip off the covers on the protocol.

RPR, however, isn't the only SONET-wanna-be killer. Lots of other technologies have their place on this murderer's row, and understanding them was simplified by the help of numerous experts. Intel's Bob Booth and Agilent's Pat Thaler clarified points in the 10 Gbits/s Ethernet spec, as did NetInsight's Christer Bohm in his explanation of DTM, which he partially invented. France Telecom's Gilles Joncour and Lucent's Dr. Stephen Trowbridge were hugely helpful in my information gathering and in understanding of OTN and OTN-related specifications.

Over in the last mile plenty of changes are occurring, and several persons helped in pulling the information together. Orckit's Yuri Gelman took the time to read through the DSL section. Mark Guzinski, project director at cable labs, offered top-notch insight into cable modem technology. Quantum Bridge's Frank Effenberger was a huge help in working through the PONs, as was SBC's Ralph Ballart.

Optical networks are far more than just infrastructure. Aside from the people already mentioned, Juniper's Ross Callon was also a big help in clearing up some holes in MPLS.

Engineers and experts—these are the folk who typically get the spotlight. Yet, a whole crew behind the scenes—public relations and marketing people—also deserves a big thanks. Here's a nod for all of their help to 3M's Holly Hassle; Crossing's Heather McCollough; Lucent's Jim Messenger, Steve Eisenberg, Wendy Zajack, and Ray Zardetto; Williams' Wendy Lea and Patty McKissick; Savvis and TSI Communications' Janice Conklin; Ebone's Olivia Harris and Rita Rabbit; IEEE's Debra Schiff; Sycamore's Christie Blake; Conexant's Angelina Lopez; Mindspeed's Carol Thornton and Roman Kichorowsky; Tektronix's Steve Kuyatt; and Orckit's Yoel Knoll.

Any project is built on a foundation and the builders also deserve mention. Thanks to Aaron, Joe, Lee, Pete, and Steve at *Data Communications* for imbuing me with a never-ending appreciation for quality journalism. Though the magazine is long gone, its rich editorial tradition carries on in the hearts of all of us who were affiliated with it.

Thanks to Andy, Steve (Steinke that is), and the rest of the *Network Magazine* staff for being patient with me as I wrote this book. One thing that makes *Network Magazine* a great place to work is the freedom Steve has given the writers to explore their areas of interest in general, and in particular has given me to explore my fascination with optics. The result is a vast and wonderful cornucopia of networking technology spanning the public and enterprises network. As for Andy, well, thanks for connecting me with Prentice Hall.

The folks at Prentice Hall have been great to work with. My editor, Mary Franz, was not only patient with my 1,001 ideas, but was constantly there as a valuable sounding board. Faye Gemmellaro, my production editor, was dynamite in shepherding the copy through the edit mill. Jerry Votta gets a big thanks on translating my scribbles (albeit with a touch of Visio) into something that resembles art. Thanks to Bruce Kenselaar for the cover and to the marketing team Bryan Gambrel, Dan DePasquale, and Mike Vaccaro for all of their help.

One of the great opportunities in this book was to blend the technology with a touch of humor. So to those ends, a big thanks to rock-climber, musician, and cartoonist supreme, Darryl Mordechai. His eye and talent made these pages far more enjoyable. Ditto to Moshe Mykoff for his writer's eye, his time, and mental space.

This project has taken a toll on everyone, not the least my family and friends. Yes, Chanani, Meira, and Yaacov, it's finally done, and thanks for being patient while Abba skipped bedtimes, working to the wee hours in the morning.

Of course, someone had to pick up the slack, and my wife, Ellen, was my rock. Without her encouragement and her handling of the home and just about everything else during the course of this writing, I couldn't have produced this book. Her editorial eye also gave me a layman's perspective on the technology. I can't thank her enough.

And a nod to the original Optical Engineer who made this book and everything else possible. Without His producing light on that initial day (and a few other things afterward), there wouldn't be anything to write about. Light really was a good idea.

DAVID GREENFIELD
Jerusalem, August 2001

Complaints, compliments, suggestions, and the like are all welcome. Drop me a line at *davegreenfield@hotmail.com.*

Part I

1 Networking at Light Speed

In this chapter...

Today's public telephone network is undergoing a metamorphosis, a change that will affect every company, indeed every individual, across the industrialized world. The change is about public network operators moving from a phone network of electrical pulses to one based on pulses of light; from a network where capacity is limited and inflexible to one where capacity is unlimited, on demand, and includes every performance characteristic that one can imagine.

Even if you don't find cables carrying trillions of bits of data as gripping as the latest Grisham novel, and bandwidth shopping isn't quite your cup of tea, the changes to the telecommunications network will still impact your life. Building out a new optical infrastructure will let carriers transport voice and data together on the same connection, enabling them to cut costs and respond to customer requests in seconds, not weeks.

So how does that affect you and me? Well, let's answer the question with a question. Did you ever need to set up a high-priority video conference on short notice? Probably not, because today's phone network requires days if not weeks to configure a circuit for the call. With intelligent optics, those connections could be established in minutes.

Or think about the situation of any local business. Take a grocery store, for example. Inventory is a huge challenge for the mom-and-pop shop. How many cartons of milk need to be ordered? What about seasonal items—how early must they be ordered to insure delivery before demand?

Not knowing those answers, proprietors end up stocking more items than necessary. Of course, those items need to be put somewhere, so either a larger store is needed or additional real estate needs to be leased or purchased—either of which incur additional real estate and utility costs.

Just-in-time delivery, where inventory ordering is automated between customer and suppliers, could help cut those expenses. However, for the medium to small company such services are often too costly and cumbersome to implement. Small companies can't afford an IT department; how will they afford the build-out of a private network with suppliers, including the necessary software and hardware to insure reliable and secure transactions?

Enter the optical network. Now even small companies can benefit from automating inventory procurement. Automated provisioned circuits enable secure private networks to be established across the Internet. The e-commerce vision can be realized. Grocery store owners will be able to go to grocerystoreowners.com and select the wholesalers with the best prices. A virtual private network (VPN)—a kind of secured highway across the Internet—can then be established with all of the suppliers. At that point application-level processes need to begin handling the complex task of giving suppliers enough access to the customer's network to insure stock fulfillment without compromising security or privacy.

Consumers, too, will benefit from the public network transformation. High-quality video conferencing, free or nearly free phone calling, and *really* fast Internet access are just some of the windfalls. Too lazy to run out and rent a video? Flip on a screen and select from a library of tens of thousands of movies! The Internet could deliver these goods with the right infrastructure.

Realizing those kinds of services, however, means more than just optics. Telecommunications operators have long realized the benefits of optics over electronics. What is needed is intelligent optics. Today, the public network is largely a second-generation optical network. Now operators are adding more capabilities and flexibility—in short, more intelligence—to their networks. Those changes will ultimately reach into corporate premises, indeed even into the very computers on the desktop, moving them toward the light.

THE PUBLIC NETWORK IN BRIEF ....

To understand the impact of optical networking, we need to get a feel for the state of the current public network. Today within the United States, dozens and even hundreds of companies fill out what we refer to as the public network—a large, amorphous conglomeration of wiring and switches connecting homes and companies around the country.

The phone network is so vast that getting a handle on it can be quite difficult. Where does one portion begin and the other end? The best approach is to think of the phone network as a system of roads. The road network consists of highways that link cities together, major thoroughfares within those cities, and smaller, residential or commercial streets.

So, too, with the public network. Between cities, long-distance operators run long-haul networks designed to carry large quantities of data over long distances. Within these long-haul networks are high-speed switching devices for moving traffic to different cities. At the edge of these long-haul networks, local providers run metropolitan networks. The metro networks consist of citywide networks, called the metro core networks, and neighborhood networks, called the metro access networks. Metro core networks are the major thoroughfares in a city linking neighborhoods together. Metro access networks link residences and business into the metro core (see Figure 1.1).

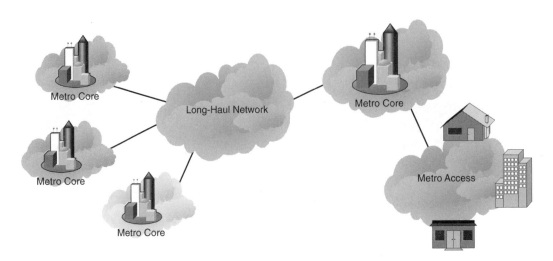

Figure 1.1
The public network consists of long-haul, metro-core, and metro-access networks.

Thirty years ago, though, the story was very different. AT&T owned and operated the long-haul and local networks. In 1984 the FCC broke AT&T up into two types of providers—the long-distance carriers or interexchange carriers (IXCs, pronounced "I-X-Cs") and seven local providers, called the Regional Bell Operating Companies (RBOCs, pronounced "are box"). The IXCs were companies like Worldcom, Sprint, AT&T and now Qwest, Global Crossing, and Level 3, who sold long-distance calling between states. The RBOCs owned the infrastructure into the home or business, called the customer premises. These dozen or so providers consolidated twice over and now consist of the following:

- Verizon (formerly GTE and Bell Atlantic)

- BellSouth

- Southwestern Bell Communications (SBC, Pacific Telesis, and Ameritech)

- Qwest Communications (formerly Qwest and US West)

With the Telecommunications Act of 1996, the RBOCs began to face new competitors. The law required RBOCs to grant regional phone companies, called Competitive Local Exchange Carriers (CLECs, pronounced "See Lecs"), access to the existing infrastructure linking up customers' locations or premises. The law also enabled CLECs to deliver phone services over new infrastructure such as high-speed wires or cable.

THE CLEC'S NIGHTMARE

Unable to compete on plain phone services, CLECs championed a combination of high-speed Internet access with telephone services—with mixed results. While using the RBOCs' existing infrastructure enabled CLECs to avoid the high material and labor costs of digging up roads and installing cables, the CLECs were left at the RBOCs' mercy. If the RBOCs refused or delayed access to their premises—which they did—the CLECs' plans were thwarted.

Nonetheless, the industry had fundamentally changed. It was now a complex web of builders and buyers, wholesalers and resellers, at times competing and at times cooperating. At the very bottom of the public network sat the wholesalers, or infrastructure owners. These companies acquired the rights-of-way from government to dig the trenches and install the cabling in the ground or across oceans. They then leased or resold whole fibers to other carriers (called dark fiber) or put on their own transmission equipment to sell some portion of the fiber's bandwidth.

Three types of operators then purchased this bandwidth. Resellers bought capacity in bulk, added their own switches, and resold the capacity in finer chunks to other users and even to smaller carriers. Switchless resellers did not own the transmission gear, reselling the capacity and the services provided by other providers. Additionally, other wholesalers bought capacity to fill out segments of their network where they hadn't laid the necessary fiber in the ground.

The Internet added a new brand of provider. Internet service providers (ISPs) specialized in enhancing raw capacity and repackaging it as Internet access. ISPs began to specialize as well. Web hosting companies emerged as specialists in housing Internet content. Application service providers (ASPs) emerged, offering access to applications on a pay-as-you-go basis. Major software providers like Microsoft, Adobe, and SAP began offering ASP service. Storage service providers (SSP) sell data storage services; managed service providers (MSP) enable companies to outsource, or contract out, the management of their networks. The acronym MSP can also refer to managed security providers, who enable companies to outsource their network security requirements (see Figure 1.2).

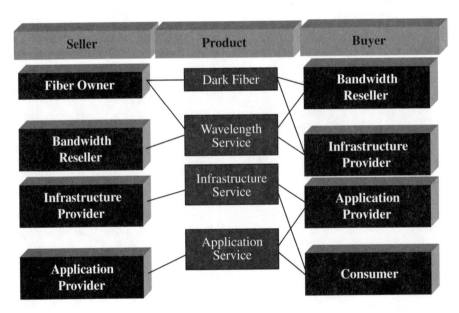

Figure 1.2
Today's telecommunications world has become a complex mesh of buyers and sellers.

TRAFFIC CHANGES ....

The diversification of the telecom marketplace created a new dynamic in terms of bandwidth pricing and traffic growth. Prices dropped dramatically while demand for more capacity soared, primarily because of the rise of the Internet.

Consider this: While voice traffic grows at about 4 percent per annum, Internet backbone suppliers cite growth in the triple digits.

Furthermore, the demand for more capacity is not localized—another big change from the old public network. Until the Internet, traffic generally could be expected to follow the 80–20 rule: 80 percent of traffic would stay local—say, within a city or a region—while 20 percent would go long-haul. Today those ratios have changed, with 80 percent of the U.S. traffic going between the top 25 cities.

All of this is compounded by the shifting nature of Internet traffic. Mass events can distort traffic flows. When Lucasfilms prereleased a trailer for *The Phantom Menace* on the Internet, for example, ISPs saw traffic requirements shift as users started pulling down the multimegabyte file. And it's not just movies—anything of mass interest can cause those kinds of changes. The Starr Report, for example, had a similar impact, as did Victoria's Secret's on-line fashion show.

OUT WITH THE OLD ....

The combination of increased competition and changing traffic requirements is pushing the bandwidth sellers to deliver their services at lower costs. This is leading to a new vision, one of a public network that seeks to deliver just enough capacity with the right transmission requirements at just the right time—exactly what the public network has been unable to do.

The problem is that the traditional phone network is based on equipment that's stuck in a kind of 20-year-old time warp, where the predominant type of traffic was circuit-switched voice calls. Back then the amount of capacity need to transport each call was well known, 64 Kbits/s. So today's equipment, called **time-division multiplexers** (TDMs), divides up a cable's capacity into neat time slots of 64 Kbits. Telephone switches sit on either end of a TDM network, taking incoming calls from consumer telephones, for example, and inserting those calls into a time slot. Those slots are mapped from one TDM to another until they reach the final switch, where the process is reversed and the call delivered to the destination.

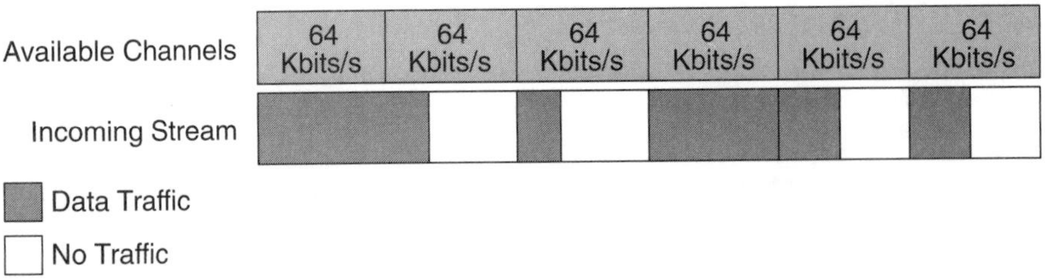

Available Channels	64 Kbits/s	64 Kbits/s	64 Kbits/s	64 Kbits/s	64 Kbits/s	64 Kbits/s

Incoming Stream

■ Data Traffic
☐ No Traffic

Figure 1.3
Data networks aren't limited by fixed 64-Kbits/s slots, so capacity ends up being wasted.

Today, however, traffic patterns have changed. Data doesn't require neat, fixed 64 Kbits/s channels like voice; it's bursty, with traffic requirements rising and dipping like a boxer. One moment 8 Kbits/s might be required; the next moment, 1 Mbit/s; and then anywhere in between (see Figure 1.3). Trying to force data flows into voice channels wastes bandwidth, as channels remain underutilized. For that matter even voice traffic has progressed to the point where 64 Kbits/s channels are a waste. Advances in voice-compression technology have squeezed voice calls into channels of 16 Kbits/s or lower.

What's more, the traditional gear used in today's networks is costly and clunky. A string of equipment from **digital crossconnects** (DXC) to **add drop multiplexers** (ADMs) to **multiplexers** are needed just to deliver a voice service. This same set of gear is needed on the receiving end as well.

On top of this cascading mess of telecom gear comes additional equipment needed for rolling out the various kinds of services. Operators will sell a wide range of services including **frame relay** and **ATM** (asynchronous transfer mode) for connecting up offices and Internet access. Each service requires separate switches, unique management systems, and specially trained personnel.

Finally, traffic requirements are shifting more rapidly than ever, while order fulfillment times need to decrease. Companies and consumers demand higher levels of service and often aren't willing to wait weeks to receive a line. The TDMs and other gear often can't respond fast enough, needing to be manually configured, which increases the time to configure—or, as you'll hear on the street, to provision—circuits.

IN WITH THE NEW ....

The answer? Simplify. Minimize the gear, slash away the service networks, and get rid of those static voice channels. In their place create a dynamic network that can be configured, or provisioned, on the fly to accommodate any type of traffic.

Developing this new network requires innovation at many levels. It means creating and deploying the underlying software and supporting hardware to accommodate the fairly static and predictable nature of voice with the bursty, ever-changing properties of data.

At the same time, developers need to find ways of creating the predictability and reliability of the traditional phone network. The phone network is built on highly resilient infrastructure capable of isolating failures within a meager 50 milliseconds. Preserving that reliability while adding all the flexibility necessary to efficiently support emerging application is no simple task. The upshot is four generations in the evolution of the intelligent optical network.

> **First Generation**—Call it the dumb era from the 80s until the mid 90s. During this time fiber was used, but only to carry a single transmission riding on top of a Sonet or SDH network. (We'll learn more about SONET and SDH in Chapter 7.) Fiber itself was treated as just another pipe, with its unique properties left largely unexploited.

> **Second Generation**—Since the late 90s optical networks have been growing more intelligent. Now, instead of just pumping one stream of data through the fiber, wave-division multiplexing (WDM) turns the fiber into a kind of virtual conduit system. Each frequency in the fiber carries a different transmissions.

> **Third Generation**—Over the next five years or so, we'll reach an era of intelligent optical networks. The old SDH/SONET gear will be gradually replaced by an optical infrastructure where data rides over the wavelength itself. There is a tight relationship between the **Transmission Control Protocol/Internet Protocol** (**TCP/IP**), the protocol underlying the and the optical gear. Requests for new IP services will automatically reconfigure the network. Instead of circuits taking several weeks to construct, they will be created within minutes with just the right traffic qualities and duration needed to support the specific transmission.

> **Fourth Generation**—Around 2015, we will see the all-optical network emerge. Nirvana has been attained. Instead of converting between optical and electrical signals, traffic remains in light form. The difference is several orders of magnitude in performance. Converting between optical and electronic, however, necessarily means a performance hit. By keeping signals entirely in optical form, mind-boggling performance becomes possible.

OPTICAL COMPUTERS..

Of course there's a fifth generation, and that's the creation of the optical enterprise. Progressively, optics begins to move down from the public network and enters the company premises. Ultimately, light makes its way into the computer itself. Computers will likely blend optical technology with electronics. The combination will make computers far faster than they are today. Some researchers estimate that problems that now take years to solve will be solved then in a matter of hours.

These systems will be particularly good at pattern recognition, much like the combination of our brains and eyes. That might sound limited, but pattern recognition is hugely powerful, affecting an amazing array of applications from inventory to detective work to child's software. Kids could, for example, get information about an obscure animal by scanning in pictures of the beast. Today's computers couldn't begin to touch those capabilities.

Building an optical computer might sound like science fiction, but in fact it's already been done. Back in 1994, a group of students led by Harry F. Jordan, Vincent P. Heuring, and Robert F. Feuerstein developed what they claimed was the first general-purpose optical computer—the Stored Program Optical Computer (SPOC). Well, general-purpose might be a bit of an overstatement. The computer could perform some basic arithmetic operations, but don't expect to start running Microsoft Office on it.

Researchers also are hard at work to develop quantum computers—computers that use atoms and subatomic particles to represent bits and bytes. What's more, a quibit (or quantum-bit) can hold multiple states, enabling quibit-based computers to perform a near infinite number of computations simultaneously.

Early optical computers, like SPOC, suffered a number of limitations, not the least of which was memory. At the time that the team created SPOC, light couldn't be slowed down or held stationary long enough for use as memory. What's more, the system was made out of a conglomeration of optical fibers, switches, and couplers, increasing complexity.

Recent developments address those challenges. Researchers have created a variety of architectures that will enable developers to reduce the size and complexity of an optical computer. **MicroElectroMechanical (MEMs)**-based devices are probably the most popular. They use a set of miniscule mirrors that can be rotated or moved at different angles to bounce light through a device.

However, optical switches today still need to convert light pulses into their electronic equivalent to determine where the data should be directed. The problem was largely that light couldn't be stored in memory. Now researchers at Rowland Institute and Harvard University have taken the first step toward creating a kind of optical memory. Both teams used the **Bose-Einstein Condensate (BEC)**, the coldest material ever created, which forms only at –460° Fahrenheit, to stop light. When a laser stimulates BEC atoms, they merge, trapping the light, and only reemitting it when the laser is turned off.

Researchers expect this technology to be used for more than just optical memory. Photonic routing, where data steams are moved around based on photons, will also benefit. Similarly, researchers expect BEC to be used in storing quibits as well to help advance quantum computing.

OPTICAL SERVICES ....

OK, back to the present. To reap the benefits of optical networking, we don't need to wait for some light-induced computing gizmo. Already the combination of fiber's huge transmission capacity with new automated provisioning systems is enabling services that may fundamentally change the way companies design their own computer networks.

These new services offer a range of bandwidths with different priorities and characteristics. Virtual cable services, for example, can link two fiber-connected offices to one another without having to pull a new cable between the offices. This is done by allocating a wavelength to link the premises. Large companies might use this service to link with their suppliers. ISPs could use this kind of service to get the lowest-priced possible connections to the Internet.

Customized optical services are another win. Suppose customers need capacity between two elements with particular characteristics. Maybe they don't want the whole wavelength, or maybe they want the wavelength's capacity with certain functionality. Now carriers can package chunks of bandwidth with different levels of protection, priority, and speeds.

LAN-to-LAN interconnect services have been around for years, but with optics the name takes on a whole new meaning. Traditionally, a LAN-to-LAN service meant connecting corporate networks through a fairly slow pipe, running at 1.5 Mbits/s versus the 10 or 100 Mbits/s speeds of the corporate Ethernet network. (Unfamiliar with Ethernet? Check Chapter 2 for a crash course.)

Now, with optical networking, LAN-to-LAN services offer speeds comparable to those of a corporate network. Customers access the carrier network through a 1 Gbit/s Ethernet interface. Exactly how much of that bandwidth they can use depends on their particular requirements. As with frame relay or ATM, they might pay for only a small portion of the capacity with the option to burst to higher speeds when necessary. As performance requirements grow, carriers can ratchet up performance to meet demands.

Finally, switched optical services enable carriers to dial up large chunks of capacity on demand, much as we do today with our telephones. A carrier might have a change in the areas of interest of its consumers. Perhaps there's a sporting event being covered and the carrier needs a couple of OC-3 pipes (2.4 Gbits/s) for a few hours. With switched optical services, a device on the customer network will hear an optical "dial tone" and be able to dial up capacity like a telephone. Of course, things are much more complicated than just a phone call—the customers need to specify things like amount of capacity, protection scheme, and the address of the end point—but the basic concept remains the same.

So what are the implications of these new kinds of optical services? Capacity on demand can enable VPNs to be configured on the fly. High-bandwidth applications, like video conferencing or video on demand, become possible.

Because of these optical services, two fundamental changes occur in the way corporate networks get built and the way carriers design their network. On the corporate side, the artificial division that's driven much of network design suddenly disappears. Until now we've assumed that traffic had to be kept local on site because the pipes between sites were either too small or too costly to accommodate corporate traffic requirements. Remember that yesterday a couple of T1s (1.54 Mbits/s) would have been considered a sizable amount of connectivity to the Internet, yet today, where users are connected via dedicated 10 Mbits/s links or shared 100 Mbits/s links, a couple of T1s doesn't look like much.

Since optical services eliminate the bandwidth bottleneck, all sorts of interesting network designs become possible. Instead of companies locating servers and the like at each location, for example, they might save on equipment costs and the IT overhead by centralizing all of the servers at a corporate headquarters, with regional offices tying back to that main office through optical links. Assuming the connections right through are at or close to LAN speeds and the distances are within reason—like across town as opposed to across the globe—users see little or no performance degradation (see Figure 1.4).

Fat pipes to the premises also open fresh new opportunities to outsource services. Instead of hiring the personnel to run storage or backup services at the corporate headquarters, for example, now they can be provided by third parties. These services have always been available in the past to very large providers for around $100,000 or more per month. What's new is the ability to deliver these services at prices of around $50 or so per gigabyte per month.

The impact on the carrier is no less dramatic. Delivery of an automatically provisioned optical network lets carriers offer whole new services, like those mentioned here. It also promises to dramatically cut the infrastructure costs of the ISPs and carriers who are purchasing the capacity from the carrier's carriers. Instead of paying for bandwidth throughout the network, they can order capacity as it's needed for as long as it's needed—just-in-time delivery, if you will, but now for the network itself.

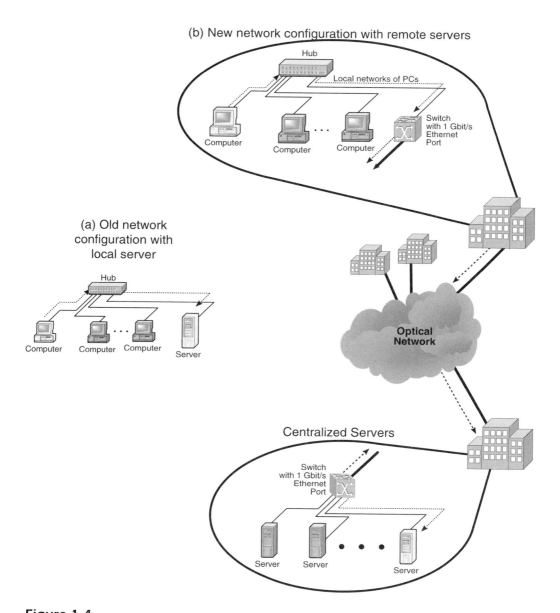

Figure 1.4
Traditional networks locate a local server at company premises (a). With optical connections to local offices, IT personnel and equipment can be centralized in one location while clients remain in their existing locations (b), cutting costs and maintaining network performance.

SHORT CUTS..

Networks are divided into corporate (or private) networks and public networks run by providers.

Deregulation in 1984 created the long-distance carriers or interexchange carriers (IXCs) and the Regional Bell Operating Companies (RBOCs). The Telecommunications Act of 1996 created competitors to the RBOCs and began to let users choose whom they would use to deliver local services. The result was a complex group of capacity providers, resellers, and buyers.

The Internet and the applications that would ride over it drove the need for higher capacity, delivered instantaneously, with differing levels of service quality. The combination of increasing competition and the Internet is leading the demand for cheap, custom bandwidth.

Traditional networks are optimized for voice, not data. The intelligent optical network can handle both equally well. It consists of long-haul networks, metropolitan core networks, metropolitan access networks, switching, and routing.

Optical deployments are varied, leading to five generations. The first generation uses fiber only as a transport. The second generation adds DWDM gear for extracting more capacity from the optical network. The third generation moves to an all-IP infrastructure. The fourth generation is an all-optical network. The final step is to develop optical computers.

There are four main types of optical services. Virtual cable services connect two fiber-connected offices through a wavelength. Custom optical services enable carriers to package chunks of bandwidth with different levels of protection, priority, and speeds. LAN-to-LAN interconnect services connect customer through a 1 Gbit/s Ethernet interface. Switched optical services enable carriers to dial up large chunks of capacity on demand.

2 The Basics of Communications

In this chapter...

Computer communication, it's been said, models the postal system. Just as the postal service devised rules on how we send our mail, so too scientists and engineers devised conventions for how computers can share information. Those rules encompass not only what defines a street address, but also the envelope's very paper stock, or (in the case of optical networking) fiber. The postal system, then, could be termed "intelligent" and able to make some pretty complex decisions about how to direct the mail. The same could be said for the world of optics.

The big difference between an intelligent optical network and optical networking is that the former is more than just fibers and couplers passing light from one point to another. Intelligent optical networking encompasses the totality of the communications system—from the applications that we might use down to the amplifiers and fiber in the ground. This network comprises optical transmission gear well as the multiplexers, routers, and switches needed to build the voice and data network on top of that transmission layer. Despite the hardware-sounding nature of it all, huge amounts of software are needed to make this inanimate mass of circuit boards intelligent—or at least as intelligent as a mentally deranged rat jacked into a blasting stereo.

To understand optical networking, then, we first need to understand the overall structures of how computer networks transmit and share information. Then we can delve into the details on fiber composition and the like. Put it all together and we'll be able to appreciate the complexity, and elegance, of light-based networks.

THE ENVELOPE, PLEASE......................................

Rules—**protocols,** if you will—determine how to properly insure that our mail travels through the postal system. Without these rules, a simple message might never reach across town, let alone across the country. This collection of rules, the postal system's communications architecture, bears a striking resemblance to the rules guiding computer communications. And like postal communications, computer communications rely on the protocols to ensure effective communication. Although many computer vendors have defined communications architectures, today two predominate. We'll begin studying these two architectures by understanding how our common postal system works. Then we'll have a blueprint for piecing together the components of the intelligent optical network.

Write a letter—an important letter perhaps, to a business associate or a dear friend. If it's important enough, you might want to encrypt the letter. You'll be sure to add the proper information to the envelope—the recipient's name, the name of his/her department, the name of the company, the city and state, the zip code, and country. You'll also be sure to attach postage to the envelope guaranteeing the necessary mail service, like regular mail or overnight delivery.

These pieces of information are the norms accepted by society for sending mail. Together they form the postal rule book, what we would call in computerese a "mail architecture," for sending letters. Computer-communications have similar if not identical norms. Today there are two widely recognized models for how computers from different manufacturers can communicate. The official model, called the International Standard Reference Model of Open Systems Interconnection (OSI), was defined by **the International Organization for Standardization (ISO)** back in the early 1980s. (The flipped letters in the acronym reflect the French spelling.) The unofficial model is that of **Transmission Control Protocol/Internet Protocol (TCP/IP)** architecture, which evolved from work on the Internet in the 60s and today runs the Internet.

Both are premised on the idea that computer communications can be divided into multiple, discrete layers. This enables tremendous flexibility, as changes to one layer are independent of the other layers. To put it another way, changes to the cost of a stamp remain independent of how you address the envelope.

Obvious? Perhaps. But until the widespread acceptance of these architectures, computer communications were guided by proprietary sets of interlocking rules that made upgrading one part of the architecture very difficult. Each mainframe and minicomputer manufacturer had its own little communication fiefdom for sharing information between its own computers. It's similar to an interoffice mail systems versus the public mail service: very effective sending mail within a company, but useless for delivering mail to someone outside of the company.

The OSI Model and TCP/IP architecture established the framework for breaking down those walls. They in many ways paralleled the whole development of the PC. Now suppliers could specialize in specific components—memory chips, processor and hard drives in the case of the PC, and various communications components in the case of OSI and TCP/IP architectures. The defined rules meant that different vendors' components could communicate, thus freeing manufacturers to specialize and evolve their respective communications components as necessary. Reality is, of course, never so neat. Interoperability problems to this day play a major role in communications. Still, this general shift in thinking did create computer networks that could be built from different vendors' equipment and enabled small startups, like Cisco, to ultimately replace IBM and DEC as the kingpins in communications.

Architectural Details

The two architectures bear a striking resemblance, with the OSI model being slightly more complex. Specifically, the OSI model consists of seven layers. The bottom layer (layer one) is the Physical layer, followed by the Data Link layer (layer two), the Network layer (layer three), the Transport layer (layer four), the Session layer (layer five), the Presentation layer (layer six), and the Application layer (layer seven). Optical networking typically covers the bottom three layers.

The TCP/IP architecture is nearly identical, except on two points. At the bottom, TCP/IP lacks a Physical layer and calls the Data Link the Link layer. At the upper end, TCP/IP combines the Application, Presentation, and Session layers into an Application layer. Both can be seen in Table 2.1, along with their respective functions and the kinds of products that would play into each category.

Table 2.1   Models of Communication

TCP/IP Model	OSI Model	Functions	Sample Products
4. Application	7. Application	Provides network services to access OSI environment	File Transfer Protocol and network management
	6. Presentation	Services for enhancing application interconnections	Encryption and text compression
	5. Session	Interconnects applications	Sockets software
3. Transport	4. Transport	Ruggedizes network interconnections	TCP software
2. Network	3. Network	Hides the nuances of the lower communications networks from the upper layers	Routers, IP software
1. Data link	2. Data link	Interconnects computers and insures reliable transport in a work group	Ethernet cards, Layer 2 switching
	1. Physical	Actual transmission of a bit on the wire or fiber—things like voltages, frequencies, and wavelengths	Cabling, fiber, connectors, amplifiers,

The layers in the OSI and TCP/IP architectures are roughly parallel to the conventions we use to send letters through the postal system. The Physical layer is akin to the mechanics needed for sending mail—where the letters should be placed for pickup, the language that should be used, how to shape the letters in the address, and where those letters should be placed. With optical networks, the physical layer describes the fibers, amplifiers, and other devices for interconnecting computing equipment. This layer also defines the how transmissions travel on the network.

The Data Link layer is like the postal workers who pick up and deliver the mail. They determine how frequently our mail is delivered and retrieved and what size packages will be accepted or rejected. This particular "algorithm" is a certain type of Data Link layer communication, a **time-division multiplexing** (TDM) solution, which we'll learn more about later, but the concept of controlling access to and insuring a reliable connection on a local network is common to all Data Link layers. Other types of Data Link layer protocols that we'll explore are **Ethernet** and **ATM** (Asynchronous Transfer Mode).

More specifically, the Data Link layer consists of two sublayers—**the media access control** (MAC) and the **logical link control** (LLC). The LLC passes packages of data together into data units or packets,[1] what could be called the networking equivalent of an envelope. The MAC defines how and when computers can transmit these packets onto the fiber and insures reliable communications within that local network. To use our analogy, the MAC operation is like a postal worker who picks up from one local address and delivers to another local address without going back to the post office. Types of MAC-oriented devices include the network adapters that connect PCs and other devices to the network, and layer-2 switches for interconnecting networks.

JEFF DISCOVERS THE SECRET OF NEXT GENERATION
OPTICAL NETWORKING - POSTAL MULTIPLEXING.

---

[1] The networking industry will use the terms packets and frames interchangeably. We'll use packets to refer to the data traveling over shared media networks, like Ethernet, and frames to refer to the packages of data used in SONET or SDH networks, or in frame relay networks.

The Network layer provides internetwork communications. It's the place where all the nonlocal mail gets delivered. Probably the best-known network protocol today is IP (as in TCP/IP), though older protocols still exist, including **IPX** (used in the older **NetWare** networks). Routers, which we will explain in greater detail later, would be the kinds of devices that use the network protocols.

The Transport layer insures the accuracy of these interpostoffice or internetwork transmissions. If any data or any mail gets lost, it's the responsibility of the transmission layer to correct that error. TCP is a Transport layer protocol.

Once the mail arrives at a home or building, it needs to get to the appropriate individual inside that building. The same goes for computer communications. Data needs to be sent to the right process inside a computer. This is the responsibility of the Session layer.

Even then, the letters within those envelopes may contain certain properties. They could be written in invisible ink, for example, for better security. They could be written on different types of paper or with different colored markers. This is the domain of the Presentation layer—to provide the necessary services, like encryption, for enhancing these interapplication communications.

Finally, people need to be able to read the actual letters. Perhaps they need some kind of instruction manual or application to guide them. The Application layer provides such various services and, in the computer world, offers interfaces to the desktop applications for accessing the different layers in the OSI or TCP/IP environment (see Figure 2.1).

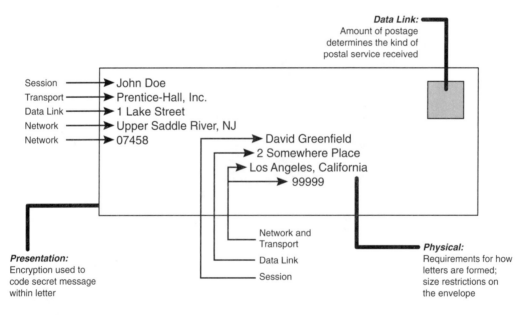

Figure 2.1
OSI model of a letter.

Bits and Bytes

When we send a message, we begin by forming the names and words that comprise the address. We then put that information into a medium that can be received by all— the words on a paper. Those words are all in English and provide certain key information for delivering the message, the name of the person, his or her location, our name and location, and the proof of the necessary postal fee.

Optical communications are no different. They need to properly address their envelopes—the data packets. The letters that they use, however, aren't the alphabet, but a complex series of optical pulses called bits. Each **bit** represents a one or a zero, an on or an off. When grouped together in sets of eight, those bits represent discrete chunks of information, characters if you will, called bytes. Actually, some networks and computer systems use ten-bit bytes, and in communications the term *octets* is often used to clearly distinguish a byte of eight pulses.

Similar to the way we shape our letters, those bits get encoded in particular ways so computers on the network will be able to understand them. Today's optical networks, and for that matter computer networks in general, use digital communications that send bits as pulses of energy, or in our case, pulses of light. Then, too, not all communications are digital. Voice communications, for example, are analog (see "Digital vs. Analog").

DIGITAL VS. ANALOG

Today's optical networks might use digital communications, but the traditional phone system used analog communications. The difference is a matter of form. The heights or levels of analog signals continuously change. Digital signals, however, are either on or off (see Figure 2.2).

Each has its benefits. Analog signals reflect the way our eyes and ears naturally work. Accordingly, building analog transmitters and receivers aimed at delivering information to our ears and eyes was easier using analog communications.

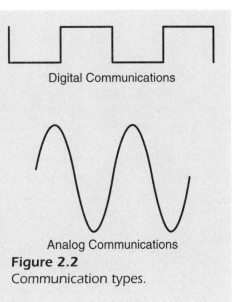

Digital Communications

Analog Communications

Figure 2.2
Communication types.

> Digital signals, however, are easier to process with electronics. Detecting whether a signal is present or not is much easier than deciphering a continuously changing analog signal. Noise or distortion on a line can easily garble an analog signal. The same can happen to a digital signal, but not as easily, typically making a digital signal a lot clearer than its analog counterpart.

Exactly how these "letters" get "shaped" or sent onto the digital network is called the *encoding scheme*. Early data networks running the Ethernet protocol, for example, used **Manchester encoding** to represent ones and zeros through transitions in the middle of a bit. Higher-speed versions of Ethernet, like Gigabit and 10 Gigabit Ethernet, use 8B/10B encoding, which changes 8-bit bytes used in computers to 10-bit bytes for transmission onto the fiber. This conversion allows additional information to be packaged into the signal and helps insure a clear signal for easy interpretation by the receiving stations.

The number of bits that can be carried across an optical or electrical communications channel is called the channel's *bandwidth*. Actually, the term is slightly confusing. Originally, bandwidth was a measure of the amount of electromagnetic spectrum used in a transmission. Ethernet, for example, uses 20 MHz (Mega-**Hertz**) to carry a 10 Mbits/s signal (see "So Just What Is a **Yotta**?"). Today, however, communications engineers use the term to refer to the carrying capacity of that channel.

SO JUST WHAT IS A YOTTA?

No, it's not the Jedi master of Star Wars fame. **Yotta**, **peta**, **kilo**, **mega**, and a host of other prefixes are standard metric nomenclature used by the Système International (SI) for abbreviating some truly mind-bogglingly long (or short) numbers. To make matters more complicated, when used with units of time (hertz per second or **megabits** per second) they represent powers of 10 as measure of data storage (megabytes) and so come in powers of 2. Here's the score on Yotta and its friends:

Frequency

1 kilohertz (KHz)	one thousand	$1,000^1$	10^3
1 megahertz (MHz)	one million	$1,000^2$	10^6
1 gigahertz (GHz)	one billion	$1,000^3$	10^9
1 terahertz (THz)	one trillion	$1,000^4$	10^{12}

1 petahertz (PHz)	one quadrillion	$1,000^5$	10^{15}
1 exahertz (EHz)	one quintillion	$1,000^6$	10^{18}
1 zettahertz (ZHz)	one sextillion	$1,000^7$	10^{21}
1 yottahertz (YHz)	one septillion	$1,000^8$	10^{24}

Data Storage

1 kilobyte	1024 bytes	2^{10} bytes
1 megabyte	1024^2 bytes	2^{20}
1 gigabyte	1024^3 bytes	2^{30}
1 terabyte	1024^4 bytes	2^{40}
1 petabyte	1024^5 bytes	2^{50}
1 exabyte	1024^6 bytes	2^{60}
1 zettabyte	1024^7 bytes	2^{70}
1 yottabyte	1024^8 bytes	2^{80}

The lengths of the waves used in optical communications are at the other end of the scale, being far shorter than a meter. Those values are:

Measure	Symbol	Value (in English)	Value (base 10)
1 decimeter	d	tenth	10^{-1}
1 centimeter	c	hundredth	10^{-2}
1 millimeter	m	thousandth	10^{-3}
1 micrometer	μ	millionth	10^{-6}
1 nanometer	n	billionth	10^{-9}
1 picometer	p	trillionth	10^{-12}
1 femtometer	f	quadrillionth	10^{-15}

The sheer scale of those numbers makes them hard to comprehend. Some practical examples can put them in perspective:*

Picometer—Size of Bohr diameter of a hydrogen atom in a ground state (106 pm)

Nanometer—Size of a virus (about 100 nm)

Micrometer—Size of bacterium (about 2 μm)

Millimeter—A little bit less than the size of a raindrop (about 1.5mm)

Kilometer—A little more than twice the size of the Empire State building (449 m)

> **Megameter**—One-third of the distance from LA to New York (3.94 Mm) or of the diameter of the moon (3.48 Mm)
>
> **Gigameter**—Roughly the diameter of the sun (1.39 Gm)
>
> **Zettameter**—The diameter of the galaxy
>
> **Yottameter**—The radius of the observable universe is 100–200 yottameters
>
> *More information about scales of these and other measurements can be found at *http://www.alcyone.com/max/physics/orders/metre.html*

The relationship between the amount of spectrum and bandwidth is defined in an algorithm called Shannon's theorem. It says that the capacity of a channel increases inversely to the amount of noise in the channel. We'll learn more about the property of waves, namely frequency, when we study light in Chapter 3, but the adventuresome can learn about Shannon's theorem now from Professor Geek (see "Professor Geek and Shannon's Theorem").

**Dr. Geek on...
Shannon's
Theorem**

Optical networking books often resort to mathematics to explain concepts—and for good reason. Mathematics is a wonderfully precise language that explains succinctly and clearly some very complex concepts. Unfortunately, if you're not fluent in math, no number of formulas will explain much of anything.

For that reason, you won't find formulas in the main body of this book. Those that can be understood through basic trigonometry or algebra have been segmented out to sidebars, where Professor Geek will explain the mathematical concepts.

Now back to the current topic. Does fiber carry infinite capacity? Well, not exactly, but it does contain far more than what we can consume at the moment. Determining how much capacity is possible in a system is calculated through Shannon's theorem, named after AT&T mathematician Claude Shannon. Shannon posited that as long as a signal's power increases, the capacity of a channel will continue to increase. This is because the signal's power continually increases relative to the signal's noise.

His theory says carrying capacity = $W * \log_2(1 + s/n)$, where W is the size of the frequency channel and s/n is the signal-to-noise ratio, or the "volume" of a signal relative to the amount of interference.

A typical *s/n* for a fiber is 20 dB or an *s/n* of 2.0. How much is that? Well, we'll cover the dB (decibels) in more depth in Chapter 4, but the lower the dB, the brighter the pulse—or, in acoustics, the louder the sound. A personal, and rather unscientific, measure puts the comfortable listening range for music at around 34 to 28 dB with loud at around 25 dB and very loud lower than that. Of course, these values are purely subjective and will vary between individuals, but they should provide a ballpark feel.

So, taking a channel of, say, 20 gigahertz, the carrying capacity would be: 20 Ghz * $\log_2(1+2)$ = 20 * 1.6 = 32 Gbits/s. This assumes, though, that systems use the simple on-off keying to represent bits of information.

If more sophisticated algorithms are employed, more bits can be encoded for each piece of spectrum, reaching the total capacity of fiber. How much is that? Recent research at Bell Labs indicates that optical fibers could at most handle 3 bits/Hz for a total carrying capacity of 150 terabits/s per fiber. By contrast, commercial transmissions today reach just 2 Tbits/s and laboratory transmissions 10 Tbits/s. So, is a fiber's capacity infinite? Well, probably not, but we probably won't reach the limits in the foreseeable future.

Network Topologies

Once bits are encoded, they get sent out on a fiber. Today fiber networks can be constructed in basically three different topologies: point-to-point links, hubs, and rings.

Point-to-point networks are the simplest types of connections, where information is sent by one station directly to the other. These may be easy to implement, but are not very reliable. A single fiber cut can break the connection (see Figure 2.3).

Figure 2.3
Point-to-point link.

Hubbed topologies join multiple point-to-point links with some device—a multiplexer, switch, or hub—in the center (see Figure 2.4). When hubbed networks are interconnected, they form a kind of meshed network (see Figure 2.5) that can offer tremendous resiliency and performance efficiencies.

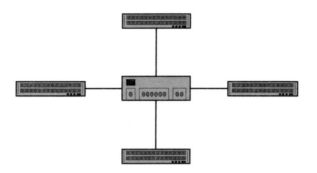

Figure 2.4
Hubbed network.

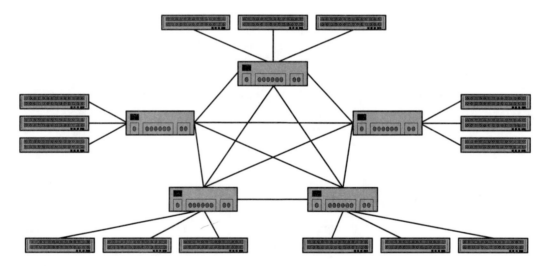

Figure 2.5
Meshed network.

Ring topologies are a compromise between the two (see Figure 2.6). They offer more resiliency than a point-to-point link and use less fiber than a hubbed network. Often rings are built in concentric circles so that, should one ring fail, traffic can be sent on the backup ring (see Figure 2.7 and "SONET Protection," in Chapter 7).

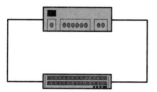

Figure 2.6
Ring network.

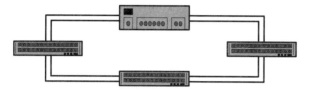

Figure 2.7
Dual ring network.

HEY, MR. POSTMAN ....

We've learned a lot about the mechanics of addressing an envelope. It's now time to look at the substance of that address, the Data Link layer. There are two basic components to getting a message across a computer network or across a mail system. There's the delivery mechanism, the postmen if you will, for transporting the message; and there's the addressing information indicating where in the network the message should be sent.

There are three basic models for how these "postmen" can function and the addressing formats that are used. Probably the simplest to understand **is wave-division multiplexing (WDM),** also called **frequency-division multiplexing (FDM)** in the analog world. With WDM, the network is conceived as a series of point-to-point links where different transmissions are sent along different wavelengths. These signals travel to a wave-division or frequency-division multiplexer, where they are combined and put onto a single cable (see Figure 2.8).

WDM would be like each building having its own personal postmen—effective, but very expensive—and if there are too many postmen, then there's quite a lot of traffic on the roads interfering with transmission. The same goes for a WDM network. Only a certain number of channels are available on the network, after which point the channels start to interfere with one another.

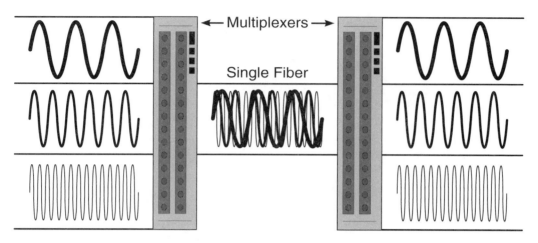

Figure 2.8
Wave-division multiplexing.

At some point a scheme for sharing a channel's bandwidth must implemented. Enter **time-division multiplexing (TDM)**. With TDM, each station sends information at a predefined interval. The interval can be established once, by reserving time slots on the networks between two devices, or dynamically. The information in the time interval is organized into frames and contains a destination address. A multiplexer combines or multiplexes these signals together onto a single line. Eventually the time slots are received by a switch, which reads the information in the frame and decides where to send the time-slot (see Figure 2.9).

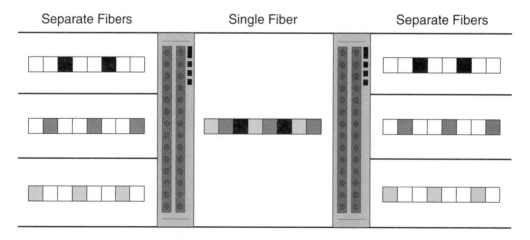

Figure 2.9
Time-division multiplexing.

TDM technologies, specifically SONET, are widely used in public networks today. The technology is highly effective in delivering voice traffic, which has very consistent bandwidth requirements and needs consistent, predictable access to the network. Think of TDM as a mailman that visits lots of buildings at a specific time each day for a specific interval of time. If the building has the same amount of mail of pretty much the same size every day, then such a scheme works well. However, if the building has tons of mail one day and no mail the next, or letters on one day and large, heavy boxes the next, the postman's resources won't be used properly.

In the third category are types of statistical multiplexing commonly found in the corporate network. With statistical multiplexing, nodes run algorithms that attempt to anticipate the traffic requirements for each device. The traffic travels on the network where it is read by an existing station or removed from the network.

There are lots of variants on statistical multiplexing (stat muxing), so simple generalizations are difficult without speaking about individual algorithms. Probably the two most significant stat muxing technologies used in networks today are Ethernet and ATM.

Ethernet

Back on May 22, 1973, two scientists, Robert Metcalfe and David Boggs, at the Xerox PARC (Palo Alto Research Center) wrote a memo describing a network they had devised to connect up the Alto, which was then a remarkable computer complete with a mouse, bitmapped display, and removable disk cartridges—items that PCs would only deliver some 15 or so years later.

The Alto may be long gone, but the network it helped inspire changed the world of data communications. Dubbed Ethernet after the ether, an imagined, gaseous substance that nineteenth-century scientists thought enabled electromagnetic waves to travel through air, the protocol has become *the* de facto standard in office connectivity.

The original Ethernet specification was something akin to buildings sending postman as necessary. Those postmen, though, all share the same car, so only one can travel back to the post office at any given time. To prevent abuse, a certain upper limit might be placed on car use. Translated into technology terms, each building or node connects to a **coaxial** cable (the road) and is marked by an **Ethernet** address. The nodes listen to the wire, and if all's clear they transmit their packets at 10 Mbits/s. These packets, the envelopes, are 1526 bytes long with a 26-byte header containing Ethernet's control information (**source address**, **destination address**, and additional framing information) and a 1500-byte **payload**. The packet travels to the destination, where it's removed from the network.

Ethernet Challenges

The idea works just fine under normal conditions, but as requirements change, all sorts of problems begin to crop up. If two buildings send their postmen at the same time, then some kind of contention scheme needs to be worked up. Easy enough—we have both postmen wait a random amount of time and then try again. Under Ethernet we call this **CSMA/CD** or collision sense multiple access/collision detection. If two stations transmit at the same time, then CSMA/CD says a collision has occurred and both need to back off a random period of time before transmitting.

But what happens if there are lots and lots of buildings or nodes? The number of collisions increases dramatically, and network performance decreases dramatically. The original Ethernet system saw the theoretical throughput of about 8 Mbits/s per station (the full 10 Mbits/s was never realized due to overhead and the like) decrease to per-station performance of about 300 Mbits/s or lower when lots of stations were added.

Other problems occur as well with Ethernet. Normal sized mail might do fine with Ethernet, but specialty mail is another matter. Priority mail, for example, or mail that might require special handling does not sit well in the everyday postal machine. The same goes for Ethernet. Normal corporate data traffic that's relatively insensitive to traffic conditions, such as email, travels along just fine on an Ethernet network. High-priority traffic is another matter. There's no innate way to insure that high-priority traffic gets delivered any faster than any other traffic. Nor does traffic that requires special handing get treated any better. Left to Ethernet alone, voice, which requires guaranteed, predictable access to the network, would have a terribly difficult time on the network. As we'll see later, we've devised various quality-of-service (**QoS**) schemes to help smooth out those problems, but the basic bumps remain.

Today Ethernet has been morphed a lot from its original inception, but much of the original protocol remains. The basic Ethernet packet formatting remains largely the same, but the wiring and performance are vastly improved. The most common type of Ethernet today, **10Base-T**, still runs at 10 Mbits/s, but over an unshielded twisted pair (**UTP**) for up to about 100 meters. Faster performance is available now over UTP with **100Base-T** operating at—you guessed it—100 Mbits/s for 100 meters. Still faster speeds are possible with **1000Base-T** running at—this is going to be a real toughie now—1000 Mbits/s or 1 Gbit/s over fiber for a couple of kilometers. Gigabit Ethernet is a leading approach for enabling corporations to access the public network. Finally, 10 Gbits/s Ethernet is now being specified for building out metro core networks (see Figure 2.10).

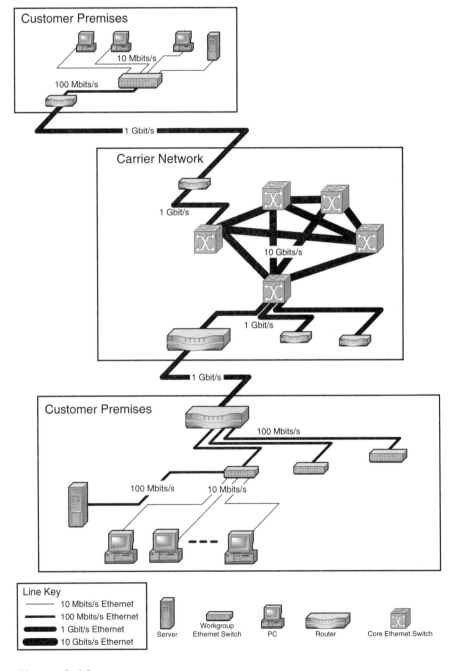

Figure 2.10
The Ethernet world.

ATM

Somewhere between the erratic nature of Ethernet and the defined structures of TDM comes **ATM (Asynchronous Transfer Mode)**. Initially conceived in late 70s by Jean-Pierre Coudreuse and an engineering team at CNET, the research arm of France Telecom, ATM was meant to be the fast track for France to launch its cable television network. It became the protocol to bring the worlds of data and voice together.

The genius of ATM lies largely in its use of fixed-length packets or cells of 53 bytes (5 bytes of header and 48 bytes of data). By eliminating Ethernet's variable packet length, ATM avoids the problems of changes in delay (called **jitter**) and minimizes delay itself, enabling the protocol to deliver predictable service, which is key for carrying real-time traffic like audio or video.

In structure, ATM differs vastly from Ethernet. For one thing, the protocol is built around a switched architecture—each node is connected back to a network of switches that rapidly connects the various devices. Cells enter the switch, their **virtual path identifier (VPI)** and **virtual channel identifier (VCI)** are read, a lookup is done in a database or table, and they're put out on the appropriate circuits on a particular port.

What's more, ATM is **a connection-oriented** protocol. This means that a connection between two points must be established across the network before data can flow. By contrast, Ethernet is **connectionless**; data is sent immediately and the network figures out how to get the packets to their destination.

Broadly speaking, two types of connections can be established—virtual circuits (VCs) or virtual paths (VPs). VCs are finer flows, typically between individual nodes, and are indicated by the cell's VCI. **Switched VCs** (SVCs) are dynamically created and torn down as required. **Permanent VCs (PVCS)** are fixed circuits. Normally, ATM services offered PVCs, with SVCs being widely implemented only in past few years.

VPs consist of several thousand VCs and are established between large units, like sites or cities. They are indicated by the cell's VPI. The big benefit of VPs comes down to scale. By switching hundreds of VPs instead of millions of VCs, providers can get much better scalability. Also, once a VP is established between two sites, it's much easier to bring up a VC.

VCs can also be characterized by the types of traffic they carry. With constant bit rate (**CBR**), cells have very predictable access to the network, just what voice and video require. Variable bit rate (**VBR**) is well suited for bursty traffic like corporate data. With VBR, a base amount of traffic is guaranteed with the option to "burst" or send more than that amount if the capacity is available. Different flavors of VBR traffic exist, called VBR-real time (RT) and VBR-non real time (NRT), to accommodate different types of traffic within that model. Available bit rate (**ABR**) circuits guarantee certain minimum level of traffic with more possible if capacity exists. Finally, unspecified bit rate (**UBR**) is a best-effort service. Traffic is carried if capacity is available but no guarantees are made. Each of these circuit types is mapped to an ATM adaptation layer (**AAL**), which converts the data traffic to the ATM cells with appropriate characteristics.

ATM suffers from two main problems, particularly in carrying data traffic. The fixed 53-byte cells don't map well onto the four-kilobyte packets generated by TCP/IP. Something called a cell tax occurs for every 50 bytes of data; some overhead results from the header and the time between cells. It's kind of like stuffing a baseball bat into lots of little envelopes strung together. It doesn't quite work. The second problem is complexity. Running IP over ATM requires an enormous amount of additional software, which companies would rather avoid.

SWITCHES, ROUTERS, AND THE LIKE.....................

Connecting lots of machines to a single network necessarily means that the capacity of that wire is split between those various computers. To improve performance and for reasons of design feasibility and network security, computer network designers began looking at ways to interconnect to reach beyond the confines of a single work group. The solutions—switching at the MAC layer and routing at the network layer—are today critical technologies for integrating the optical layer with the data traveling over it.

Two solutions were contrived—one for connecting at the Data Link and the other at the Network layer. The key to both is the delay game. The one thing network designers want to avoid is slowing the packet's path through the network. Despite the tremendous speeds of these systems, delay quickly accumulates. As delay increases, files take longer to be retrieved from across the network, and real-time applications, like voice or video conferencing, can grind to a halt.

Data Link layer switching is generally the way to connect for optimum performance. Like their physical counterparts that we'll discuss in Chapter 6, Data Link layer switches connect three or more networks together. The difference, of course, between physical layer switches and Data Link switching is one of intelligence. Physical layer switches direct information between ports without searching the contents of the data stream. They effectively appear like a fiber or cable to the higher layers and most importantly do nothing to increase network capacity.

Not so with Data Link switches. These nifty devices segment one network into multiple Data Link networks. A 12-port Ethernet switch, for example, turns one Ethernet network into 12 networks, effectively increasing the theoretical overall network bandwidth from 10 to 120 Mbits/s (see Figure 2.11). Actually, the performance is even higher. The same group that specified Ethernet specified **Duplex-Ethernet**,

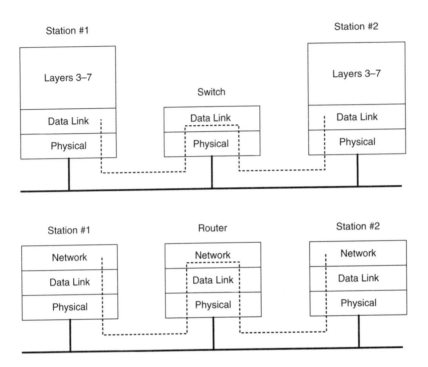

Figure 2.11
Switch and router differences

which splits the standard Ethernet network into a send and a receive channel. This enables the network to avoid collisions and lets the clients come much closer to reaching standard Ethernet's 10 Mbits/s theoretical maximum (see Figure 2.12). The upshot then isn't overall network bandwidth of 120 Mbits/s. It's 240 Mbits/s.

Switches work this magic by inspecting the MAC address on incoming packets, quickly checking a database to see whether the destination is on the network, and if not, removing the packet and sending it on to the appropriate port. Think of them as miniature post offices, where workers need look only at a street address to forward a letter and not at the city, state, and country. Since they have to look only into the MAC address, which is at the beginning of the packet, they're fast and cheap.

In fact, they are so cheap that switches change the definition of a work group. Ten years ago the work group consisted of 25 to 30 computers. As switching technology improved, fewer and fewer computers shared individual switched-Ethernet ports. Today, it's not unusual for individuals to be plugged directly into an Ethernet switch.

Being smart is another matter, though. Switches can't "see" beyond the Ethernet networks to which they are attached. If there's a network failure and a line goes down, pure switches won't pick up on it. What's more, because they're limited to the MAC

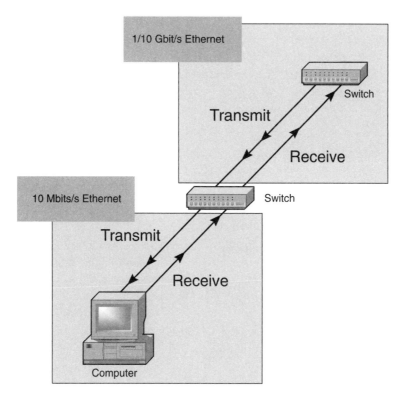

Figure 2.12
With duplex operation the transmit and receive signals are on two different pairs of wire or fiber. Originally adopted for 10 Mbits/s, duplex operation is now used in higher-speed Ethernet standards as well.

layer, enforcing security isn't their strong suit. Many hacker attacks use the network layer to which the switches are blind. Finally, if you were trying to connect two different types of networks, say Ethernet and the public network, switches wouldn't deliver very effectively. They aren't great at converting between media-types, say between the Ethernet and TDM-based networks.

Enter the routers. These devices connect networks at the Network layer. They inspect the network address on incoming packets, quickly checking a database to see with which port the network is associated, and then forward the packet appropriately. They're more like the post office operating on the level of a city and state and not a street address.

This routing decision is based on a kind of topology map of the network. The information needed to build this map is gathered from other routers via what's called **routing protocols**. Within the Internet today, ISPs commonly use the **OSPF** (open shortest path first) routing protocol for their own networks and **BGP** (border gateway protocol) to communicate between networks. Since they contain maps of the network, routers can be more intelligent in directing packets than switches. Routers can, for example, divert packets around a failed link a few routers (called hops) away.

Operating at the Network layer has other benefits and drawbacks. On the one hand, routers are able to connect different types of networks. On the other hand, routers are typically slower than switches, though modern routing technology has certainly narrowed that gap. As we'll see in Chapter 10, the next-generation routing being deployed in today's public networks combines the speed of MAC layer switching with the functionality of routing.

QoS AND VLANS ....

Chopping up bandwidth between machines, or sites, is just one part of the problem in creating an effective communications network. The type of bandwidth that's provided is another issue. Since today's traffic comes in different types and flows between different computers or sites, networkers need ways to segment network capacity and insure security. Within the TDM world this is naturally provided by the technology, but within the world of data, new schemes are needed to insure secrecy and service quality.

Up until now, we've generally thought about data networks, like Ethernet, as a single postman (or postwoman) collecting the mail of a given number of sites on, say, a single block. But what happens if those offices send lots of private mail between sites? There are natural concerns that the mail might be intercepted and read.

To prevent that from occurring, network managers within corporate networks, and increasingly carriers within the public network, implement virtual LANs (**VLANs**). VLANs tag packets as belonging to a custom-defined user group. Within the public networks, VLANs can be used to separate different customers' traffic. They can be thought of as splitting up a postal route between different companies' postmen.

Today the scheme widely used within the Ethernet world for VLANs is from the IEEE 802 group called **802.1q**. However, other technologies have or may be developing their own schemes. As we'll see later, a new metro protocol, **resilient packet ring (RPR)**, may carry its own VLANs scheme.

Within a particular virtual network carriers need be able to deliver different types of quality of service (QoS). Think of the types of applications that dominate the Internet today. Email. The Web. Instant messaging. File transfer. They are relatively tolerant to changing the Internet's traffic conditions. If a network is congested and your email is delayed, that Web page might take a bit longer to download, but no harm is done.

Now think about the times you might have tried Internet-based voice or video conferencing. Sure, it *might* work, but the quality just isn't there. Would you consider putting your business on voice traffic carried over the Internet? Probably not.

So why is it that the voice network can deliver such clear telephone calls, but the data network seems so lost when it comes to that application? The issue is a matter of quality of service. Not all traffic that gets sent onto an network can be treated the same way. Some types of applications, video or voice, carry very stringent networking requirements—low latency (delay), low jitter (delay variation), high bandwidth requirements, and high-sensitivity to loss of traffic. Other applications, like email, are relatively immune to these kinds of changes.

What's more, even within specific applications there's often a need to decide who gets access to the network first. A rough corollary might be that everyone should have access to the postal system, but first class mail should come first.

The answer, then, is to develop some way to insure that applications receive the bandwidth they require. SONET does this by pinning up the bandwidth through the entire network. Once a circuit is created between two points, time slots are reserved along the entire path (see Chapter 7). Not very efficient, perhaps, but very effective at delivery high-quality services.

Within the world of packets, implementing QoS is more complicated. Bandwidth isn't pinned up across the entire network, but instead algorithms need to be implemented at the ingress (the entrance point) to a network that will implement QoS. This might sound simple, but it actually gets pretty complicated, involving five areas.

The first is to label or tag the traffic for a particular service class. Incoming traffic into a router or switch needs to be considered, a policy checked, and then the traffic marked with a certain service level, depending on customer requirements. This might be something like gold, silver, or bronze service, where gold receives the highest priority and costs the most, bronze the lowest priority and costs the least, and silver somewhere in between.

Once the traffic is labeled, it needs to be placed in a particular queue, or memory bank, for delivery onto the network. Nonprioritized networks use first in-first out (FIFO) queuing, where the router or switch simply sends out packets onto the network as they are received. **Priority queuing** places packets of different priorities in different queues giving the highest-priority queue preferred access to the network. **Custom queuing** gives traffic classes a predetermined amount of line capacity by assigning varying amounts of queue space to each traffic class and then servicing those queues one after another. Finally, **weighted fair queuing** ensures predictable service among traffic classes. Low-volume traffic gets preferential treatment, being sent as soon as possible. Once the low-volume traffic is finished, the remaining capacity is split between high-volume traffic.

Now that the traffic is labeled, queued, and delivered onto the network, we might think that the job of QoS is completed, but in fact three more "management" steps need to be implemented. We need to police, or insure, that devices comply with the QoS definitions. There also needs to be some kind of discard method—for two reasons: (1) to drop packets from high-volume senders, and (2) to reallocate bandwidth to other users until the congested condition clears. Finally, there needs to be a way to extend these QoS features across networking technologies.

Fully implemented, QoS algorithms go a long way toward enabling carriers to develop a single network that can carry a wide range of data types. The challenge, however, particularly with IP networks today, is that while carriers might be able to label traffic as it enters the network, they can't always guarantee the proper handling of bandwidth within the core of the network, which is why MPLS was so critical. We'll learn more about traffic engineering with MPLS in Chapter 10.

SHORT CUTS..

Computer communications consists of a collection of rules, called protocols. Collectively, a set of communication protocols are known as architectures. The best known, defining a nonproprietary network, are the TCP/IP and OSI architectures.

The OSI Model consists of seven successive layers: the Physical layer, the Data Link layer, the Network layer, the Transport layer, the Session layer, the Presentation layer, and the Application layer. Intelligent optical networking deals mostly with layers one and two and, to some extent, layer three.

Optical networks use digital communications, where information is sent as series of optical pulses or bits. Analog communication is used in the phone network, particularly to conect the phones in our homes.

The number of bits that can be carried in a given amount of spectrum is predicted by Shannon's law.

Networks can be organized in three topologies: point-to-point links, hubs, mesh, and rings.

These networks are shared via three types of multiplexing schemes. Wave-division multiplexing (WDM) sends information on different wavelengths. Time-division multiplexing (TDM) sends information at different time intervals. Statistical multiplexing, like Ethernet and ATM, sends information as needed.

Ethernet dominates in the corporate networks and SONET in the public network.

There are two ways to interconnect Ethernet networks. Switches connect at the Data Link layer. Routers connect at the Network layer.

QoS and VLAN functionality are needed to deliver a mix of data and voice traffic between nodes securely. QoS is a scheme by which bandwidth and the proper traffic parameters are provided for carrying a specific type of data.

VLANs tag packets as belonging to a custom-defined user group. Within the public networks, VLANs can be used to separate traffic of different customers over a common network.

Part II

3 Fundamentals of Light

In this chapter...

The idea of using light to represent data isn't particularly new. Over a hundred years ago, Alexander Graham Bell demonstrated that light could carry voice through the air. What *is* new, however, is the ongoing improvement of the fibers and other basic optical components. While scientists in the '60s predicted that fibers would be limited to 500 meters, today's optical pythons can reach 1000 times that distance.

Those improvements are made possible by an understanding of light's basic properties. Reflection and refraction play critical roles in enabling light to travel down a fiber, while scattering becomes important on extended lengths of fiber.

The irony is that, while scientists know how light behaves, they are less clear on what comprises light. Experiments show that light can be explained both as a particle and as an electromagnetic wave, a form of energy caused by the excitation of an atom's electrons. Both explanations will be important to our understanding of optical networking.

ATOMS, ELECTRONS, AND THE LIKE.....................

Until the 19th century, light was conceived as a series of particles emitted by some object and in turn viewed by another object. The **particle theory of light**, as its called, largely stems from the Newtonian understanding of light that stretched back to the Greeks who dubbed these tiny particles corpuscies. Under the Newtonian understanding proposed in 1666, light was a series of particles emitted by a light source that stimulated sight in the eye. By conceiving light as a series of particles, Newton was able to explain reflection and refraction.

Even within Newton's lifetime, however, the particle theory was challenged. In 1678, Christian Huygens, a Dutch physicist, argued that reflection and refraction could also be explained by understanding light as a wave. Huygens' views were rejected at the time by opponents who argued that if the **wave theory** were true, light should bend around objects and we should be able to see around corners. As we'll see later, light in fact does bend around corners—what we call diffraction—though it isn't easily observable because light waves have short wavelengths.

The wave theory of light laid largely dormant for just over a century when in 1801, Thomas Young, a British physicist, physician and Egyptologist (who also helped decipher the Rosetta Stone that led to the understanding of Egyptian hieroglyphics), first demonstrated light's wave properties. Young's experiment proved that light rays interfere with one another, a phenomena unexplainable under the particle theory as no two particles could inhabit cancel each other out. Additional research during the 19th century, gradually swayed the scientific community towards viewing light as a wave that passed through an invisible substance, called ether, the same substance after which Metcalfe named the popular local area network, Ethernet (see Chapter 2).

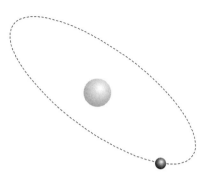

Figure 3.1
Classical view of the atom.

    This theory, that light is a wave, can be easy understood by using the atomic model proposed by Ernest Rutherford (1871–1937), the "layman's" view of the atom. With the Rutherford model, the electron's orbit around a nucleus, comprised of protons and electrons, like planets orbiting around the sun. The nucleus exerts a force, the electric force, on the electrons, holding them in their respective states (see Figure 3.1). The closer an electron is to the nucleus, the greater the attraction. The area of, shall we say, "reach" of the protons is called the force field (in physics, not Trekkian, terms). Positive charges placed in this field are repelled by the protons; negatively charged particles, like electrons, are attracted.

    As energy is introduced, the electrons are excited and begin to vibrate in their place. The electrons' vibrations distort the electric field holding them, forming an electromagnetic wave (see Figure 3.2).

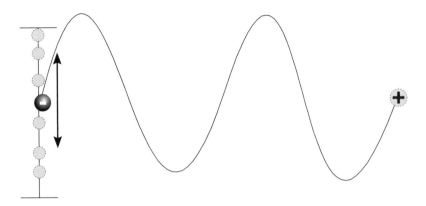

◯ Electron's Future Location
⬤ Electron's Current Location

Figure 3.2
Under the classic view, electromagnetic waves are formed when an electron vibrates, causing a distortion in the electric force field exerted by a positively
charged particle.

Quantum View

With their understanding of wave coupled with their understanding of electricity and
magnetism, 19th century scientists were able to explain most known properties of
light. Yet some phenomena, notably the **photoelectric effect**, could not be explained.
A new model was to be developed, the quantum model of light, that combined elements of both particles and waves.

Under the photoelectric effect, electrons can be released when light strikes a
semiconducting material. Using the wave theory of light, the kinetic energy of the released electron should increase with the intensity of the light. Experiments, however,
showed that the amount of additional energy was independent of the light's intensity.

It was only until the start of the 20th century that this problem was solved. Albert Einstein proposed a theory based on Max Planck's theory of quantization, which
assumes energy to be present in a light wave in packages, called photons. Einstein the-
orized that the energy of these photons is proportional to the frequency of the electromagnetic wave.

Using Plancks original quantum theory and Einstein's conception of light as a
series of photons, Niels Bohr in 1913 introduced a new model of the atom to replace
the Rutherford model. The problem with Rutherford's model is that if energy is produced though an electron's vibrations, then according to this model electrons should

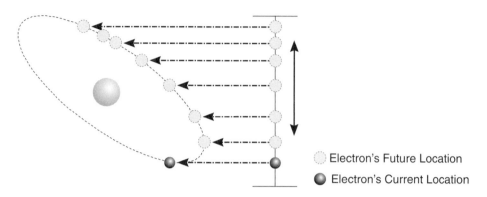

Electron's Future Location

Electron's Current Location

Figure 3.3
An electron's orbit appears the same as an electron vibrating in place, which under the classic view should lead to an electromagnetic wave.

be emitting energy all the time. Do you see why? When you map an electron's orbit onto a two-dimension plane the electron appears to be constantly vibrating, because in fact it is! (see Figure 3.3).

This means, then, that according to the conservation of energy, the electron would slow down each time energy was emitted. After enough time, the electron would be unable to hold its position, eventually crashing into the nucleus, destroying the atom. Matter would exist for a fraction of a second and this book would never have been written.

Bohr postulated that classical radiation theory doesn't hold for atomic-sized systems. He thought that that electrons were contained at certain energy levels around the nucleus. The term *energy levels* is used for many reasons, one of which is that although electrons might appear to move, they don't actually orbit around the nucleus (see Figure 3.4).

Whereas classical physics allowed for nearly any orbit, the quantum view says that only "special" energy levels are possible. Electrons are pushed to higher energy levels through particles of light, called **photons**, sharing the same frequency. When the electron drops from a higher energy level to a lower one, it emits a photon equal to the energy difference between the two states. When enough photons are emitted of the right frequency, visible light is produced.

The quantum understanding of light view might sound much like the original particle view and, in fact, there is a strong similarity to the quantum model. What's important here though is that Einstein's theories contain aspects of both the wave and particle theories. The photoelectric effect then results from the energy transfer of a single photon to an electron in the metal. Yet this photon's energy is determined by the frequency of the electromagnetic wave.

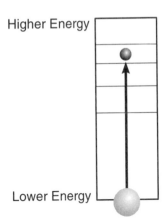

Higher Energy

Lower Energy

Figure 3.4
Under Bohr's model, electrons are shown as inhabiting different energy states;
the farther they are from the nucleus, the more energy they contain.

So is light a particle or wave? It's both, or perhaps more accurately, light exhibits qualities of both particles and waves depending on the situation. Much of optical networking can be explained with the wave theory of light. We'll resort to the particle theory where necessary.

LIGHT FINALLY CONFRONTS ITS
WAVE-PARTICLE DUALITY

PROPERTIES OF WAVES...

As a type of **electromagnetic radiation**, light falls into the category of transverse waves. With **transverse** waves, components oscillate perpendicular to the motion of the wave. Anybody who has spent time at the beach, for example, knows all about transverse waves and their perpendicular motion. Water waves are a good analogy for what happens with electromagnetic waves. As a water wave rolls toward the shore, swimmers bob up with its crest and down with its trough. This is what we mean by perpendicular motion.

Not all waves are transverse. With **longitudinal** waves, the components of the wave oscillate or vibrate in parallel to the wave's direction. As an example, think of a coil spring. Pulling it out and pushing it back causes its components to compress.

Like ocean waves, electromagnetic waves move together in a series. Imagine yourself hovering above the ocean, looking down at the wave. What you might see looks a like a series of ridges in the water (see Figure 3.5). The lighter areas are where waves peak and the darker areas where they fall. This series of waves is called a wave train. The direction of the wave train is indicated by drawing a ray across the waves' peaks.

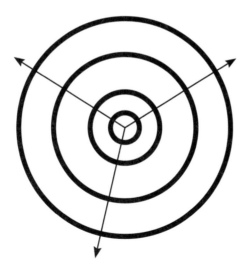

Figure 3.5
The direction of the wave train is indicated by the three rays.

Look at a wave train in profile and you get a sine wave with certain distinct properties of height, length, frequency, and speed. The height or amplitude of the wave is measured from the wave's peak, or crest, to the axis around which the wave moves. The amplitude is also a measure of the brightness of the pulse. The distance between the successive troughs of the waves is the **wavelength**. The ability of DWDM systems to use signals of different wavelengths to carry different transmissions has enabled providers to dramatically increase the capacity of their fibers (see Figure 3.6).

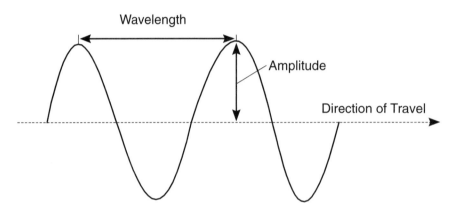

Figure 3.6
Viewed in profile, an electromagnetic wave has a sinusoidal form.

The number of times a wave oscillates each second, or it's **frequency**, is measured in hertz (Hz) after Heinrich Hertz, the physicist who discovered radio, not the car rental company. A hertz refers to a complete cycle—starting where the wave begins its rise and fall. The number of times a cycle crosses a particular point in space, which is the inverse of frequency, is called the **period**.

If two waves arrive at their crests and troughs at the same time, they are said to be in **phase**—or, to put it another way, waves that are in phase appear symmetrical. Similarly, if two points on a wave are separated by whole measurements of time or of wavelength, they are also said to be in phase (see Figure 3.7).

Another important property of light is its speed. The speed of a wave can be calculated by multiplying frequency and wavelength. Since all electromagnetic waves travel at the speed of light, which in a vacuum is 299,792,458 meters per second or around 300,000 kilometers per second, only frequency or wavelength needs to be known. The constant speed of light yields an inverse relationship between frequency and wavelength. The higher the frequency, the shorter the wavelength.

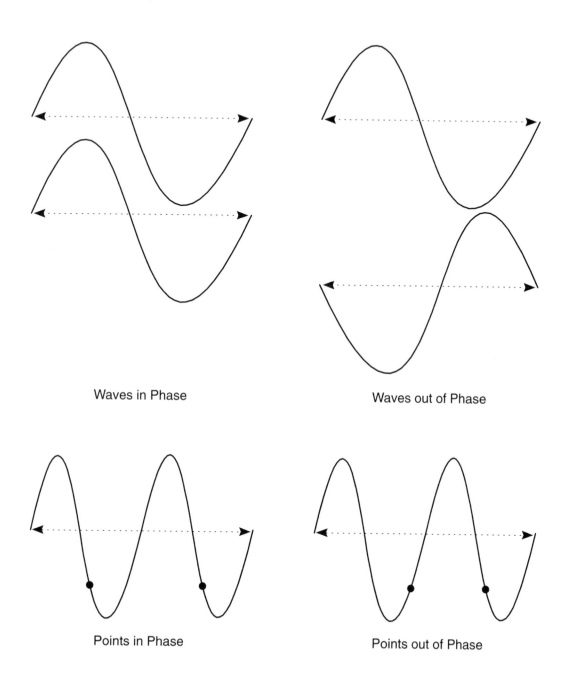

Waves in Phase

Waves out of Phase

Points in Phase

Points out of Phase

Figure 3.7
Phase in waves and points.

Actually, referring to an electromagnetic wave as a sinusoidal wave is a simplification. Electromagnetic waves are called as such because they consist of electrical and magnetic fields moving orthogonally, or at right angles, and in phase with one another. Since the two fields normally do not interfere with one another, only the electrical component is shown.

ELECTROMAGNETIC SPECTRUM ....

By understanding frequency and wavelength, we can understand where on the electromagnetic spectrum optical communications occur. The spectrum represents the range of electromagnetic phenomena. At one end sit gamma rays (around 1 ZHz), the kind of radiation released in a nuclear blast, and at the other end are radio transmissions (1 KHz to 1 GHz). Optical transmission happens just above visible light and below the ultraviolet band. There's some overlap in these regions, as the divisions in the spectrum are entirely manmade (see Figure 3.8).

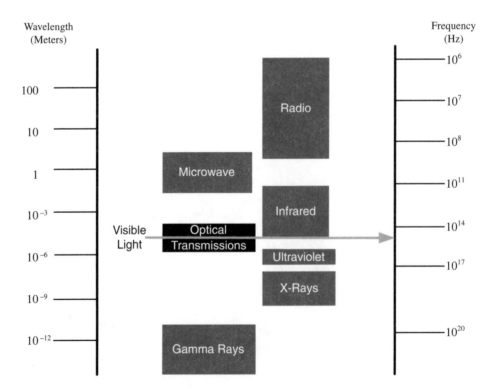

Figure 3.8
The electromagnetic spectrum.

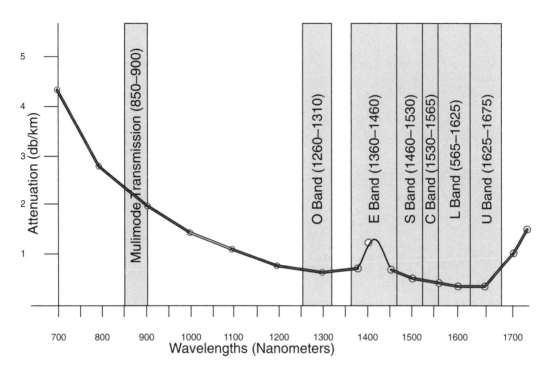

Figure 3.9
The transmission bands.

To promote interoperability between optical equipment, the International Tele-communications Union (ITU), the standards body responsible for global telecommunications standards, defined six bands for long-distance optical communications. A seventh band is used for short-haul transmissions (Figure 3.9).

WAVE BEHAVIOR..

When waves move through a medium, they exhibit certain key characteristics—key because they have implications for the optical system. These characteristics cover **reflection**, **refraction**, **interference**, and **diffraction**.

Start with the most commonly known characteristic, reflection. When waves hit a surface, they bounce back. No surprise there. Look into a mirror and you can see reflection at work. In fact, nearly all objects reflect some light. The color that we see is light reflected off an object.

When light strikes a surface, it bounces off at a particular angle. This angle, the **angle of reflection**, is equal to the angle at which the ray of light struck the object as

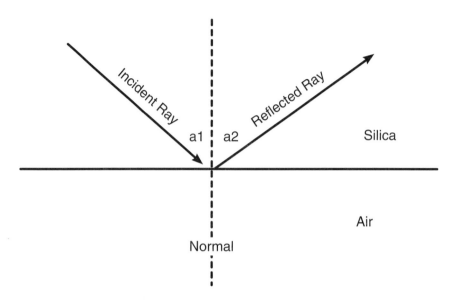

Figure 3.10
The angle of incidence (a1) equals the angle of reflection (a2).

measured from the **normal**—an imaginary perpendicular line crossing the point of intersection between the ray and the surface (see Figure 3.10).

NORMALITY—WHO NEEDS IT, ANYWAY?

At first glance, the normal—the imaginary perpendicular line used as a reference for calculating reflection and refraction—seems extraneous. Why not just measure the angle from the surface of the object being struck? The problem becomes what to do when light strikes a substance that's not flat, such as a curved sheet of glass. Then there's no common reference surface to work from. Hence the need for normality.

Reflection is of two types. In **specular reflection**, parallel light rays strike a surface and reflect off in parallel. As we'll see, specular reflection is important in understanding how waves propagate down a fiber. **Diffuse reflection** occurs when parallel rays are reflected off a rough surface at different angles, causing distortion. When fibers are crimped and **microbends** in the fiber are introduced, diffuse reflection becomes a major problem.

REFRACTION ....

Not all substances reflect light, though. Some allow portions of the light to pass through them, albeit with a bit of distortion. Put a rod into water and notice how it appears to bend. The phenomenon, **refraction**, occurs because of the change in speed as waves pass from one substance, in this case air, to another substance, in this case water.

Refraction is a very handy property when it comes to optics. In fact, it holds the answer to how a normally transparent substance, like glass, can contain an optical signal. To understand this more fully requires understanding the **refractive index** (normally referred to as n and in this book as RI). The refractive index is the ratio of the speed of light in a vacuum to the speed of light in a material. Since light always travels slower in material than in a vacuum, the RI for a substance is always greater than 1.0. RI varies depending on wavelength. Generally, the shorter the wave, the higher the RI, the slower the wave travels through the substance, and the more the wave will bend in the substance. When an RI value is cited for a substance, it is commonly done at a default wavelength, 589 nm, the wavelength of yellow sodium light (see Table 3.1).

Table 3.1　Refractive Indices for Common Substances*

Substance	RI	Substance	RI
Air	1.0003	Carbon Dioxide	1.0005
Cladding	1.49	Fused Quartz	1.46
Glass, crown	1.52	Water	1.33
Diamond	2.42	Ice	1.31

Values are for light operating at 589 nm as reported in Serway/Beichner, "Physics for Scientists and Engineers with Modern Physics," 5th ed., p. 1017.

The key here is the density of the substances. When a wave travels into a denser material, its speed and wavelength decrease, causing it to bend toward the normal. As the wave travels into a medium where its speed increases, its wavelength also increases, and the wave is bent away from the normal (see Table 3.2).

Taken together, the RI for two materials can be used to compute the angle of refraction, the amount the waves bend as they enter the new substance. This formula is called Snell's law, after the Dutch mathematician Willebrod van Roijen Snell (1580–1626).

Table 3.2   Principle of Refraction

Travels from	Travels to	
	High RI	Low RI
High RI		Wavelength increases; light waves bent toward the normal
Low RI	Wavelength decreases; light waves bend away from the normal	

Dr. Geek on...
Snell's Law

So how do you figure out how much light will bend when it travels through a substance? To find out use Snell's law, which states:

$$RI_1 * \sin A = RI_2 * \sin B$$

where:

RI_1 = refractive Index for the original substance

A = angle at which the light strikes the new substance measured from the normal

RI_2 = refractive Index for the new substance

B = angle the light will take in the new substance measured from the normal

There's an interesting phenomenon with Snell's law. As the **angle of incidence** increases, the angle of refraction also increases. At some point the angle of refraction is so great that refraction doesn't occur any more, and the incident ray is reflected back into the original substance. This angle is the **critical angle**, and the phenomenon is **total internal reflection** (see Figure 3.11).

Dr. Geek on...
the Critical
Angle

At some point, when light shines from a substance with a higher RI to one of a lower RI, the light remains in the originating substance. This angle is called the critical angle. Determine that angle through a formula derived from Snell's law:

critical angle = arcsin (RI_1/RI_2)

where RI_1 is that of the substance the light is traveling through and RI_2 is that of the new substance the light is entering.

Total internal reflection is the magic that lets light effectively travel down a fiber. As long as the signal strikes the fiber's walls at an angle greater than the critical angle

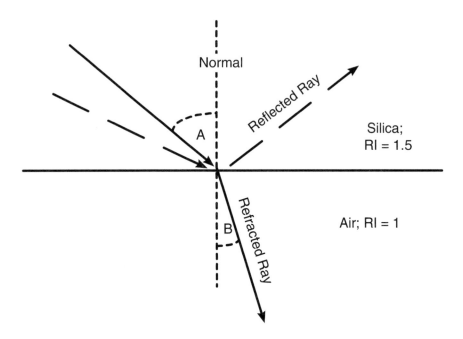

Figure 3.11
When light travels from a substance with a higher RI (silica) to one of a lower
RI (air), the ray is refracted and bent toward the normal. However, at a certain angle, called the critical angle, the light is reflected back into the originating substance (silica). This phenomenon is called total internal reflection.

(as measured from the normal) the light remains inside the core. Given that the angle
of incidence equals the angle of reflection, the signal will continue to strike the fiber
wall at a sufficient angle to travel down the fiber.

INTERFERENCE

When two waves collide, they can either amplify the signal creating a brighter pulse
or interfere with one another. When they are in phase they amplify the signal in a phenomenon called constructive interference.When the signals that are out of phase collide, destructive interference occurs and the signal is weakened (see Figure 3.12).

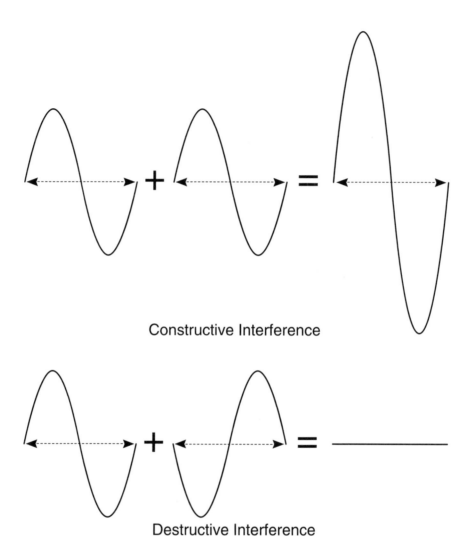

Constructive Interference

Destructive Interference

Figure 3.12
Interference can amplify or diminish a signal.

DIFFRACTION AND SCATTERING...........................

It might make sense that waves travel in straight lines, but different conditions can cause them to change. One change occurs when light encounters another substance and is diffracted. The principle is straightforward enough to understand, and it plays a major role in how light travels down single-mode fibers, where the aperture is very small.

Diffraction occurs when a wave strikes an item shorter than its wavelength at which point the wave bends. The closer the aperture is to the wavelength, the greater the diffraction effect (see Figure 3.13).

If light runs into other molecules, an effect called scattering can occur. Part of the light is deflected or scattered in different directions. How much of the light is scattered, and in which directions, depends on the type of scattering involved. We'll learn more about scattering when we study nonlinear effects of light propagating down a fiber.

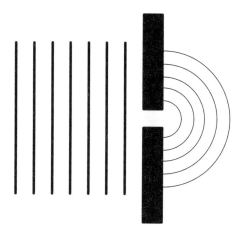

Figure 3.13
Diffraction through a narrow aperture.

SHORT CUTS..

Light is a type of electromagnetic radiation that consists of particles (called photons) or waves. Photons are emitted when electrons fall from a state of higher energy to one of lower energy. Waves are caused by the electrons' vibrations.

There are two types of waves, transverse and longitudinal. Components of a transverse wave move perpendicular to the wave's motion; those of a longitudinal wave move parallel to the wave's motion.

Light is a transverse wave consisting of amplitude, wavelength, frequency, and speed. The wavelengths of the kinds of light used in optical transmission range from around 850 to 1600 nm.

Light waves have a number of characteristics. Those critical to optical networking are reflection, refraction, diffraction, and interference.

The refractive index (RI) is a measure comparing the speed of light in in a vacuum compared to the speed of light in a substance, such as glass. The higher the RI, the slower the signal travels through the substance.

When light passes from a substance of a lower to one of a higher RI, it bends. Snell's law says that at some point the light will strike the substance with the higher RI at so great an angle that it will bounce off, as if reflected from a mirror. This phenomenon is called total internal reflection.

4 Fiber Optic Cabling

In this chapter...

If computer communication models postal communication, then the optical transport is equivalent to the conveyor belts within a postal office over which our mail moves—it's just as fundamental.

The rapid growth of the Internet pushes providers to deploy higher-speed connections. Enabled by high-tech fibers, long-distance transmission rates have grown from 2.5 to 10 Gbits/s to 40 Gbits/s. Part of the reason for the jump has been improvements in fiber optics production processes—especially in removing impurities within the core and cladding, where the light is actually carried.

These two components largely define the major cabling types: multimode and single-mode fibers. Enhancements to these two basic types addressed numerous problems that originally limited transmission distances.

WHY FIBER? ....

Any attempt to understand the underlying optical network begins with the benefits of fiber. Why the move to fiber-based networks? The immediate answer of course is capacity, but the benefits of fiber go much deeper than just capacity. They include security, resilience, and range as well.

- **Capacity**—Fiber optics offer substantially higher capacity than copper cabling. Coaxial cabling carries about 2000 analog voice calls, assuming each call runs 64 Kbits/s or around 125 Mbits/s. Top measures are difficult on fiber, because so much of the research is focused in part on range; however, during March, 2001, NEC Corporation reported being able to transmit roughly 10.9 terabits/s over 117 kilometers/s—a capability over 80,000 times that of copper cable.

- **Cost**—The increased capacity of the optical systems means that costs for producing fibers are also substantially lower than those of copper systems. The costs of laying the fiber are also reduced, because the fiber is so much smaller and lighter than copper cabling. A fiber can weigh several ounces per foot and measure a half an inch in diameter, whereas a copper cable can weigh several pounds per foot while measuring several inches in diameter. The larger size means that fewer cables can fit into a wiring duct.

- **Range**—Fiber optics can transmit data substantially further than copper cables without requiring the use of equipment to regenerate and re-time the signal. With ultra long haul optic technology, for example, signals can reach 1,500 to 2,000 kilometers before regeneration, significantly reducing the cost of the link.

- **Imperviousness to electrical noise**—Since fiber does not use an electrical connection, it has high imperviousness to noise. The system does not radiate noise nor is it susceptible to electrical noise, which can distort a signal. This means that fiber cables can be placed near a power cable, a generator, or in any other environment where there's a lot of electrical noise without incurring significant signal distortion.

- **No electrical connection**—Similarly, since fiber does not rely on electrical interfaces, working with fiber cabling is substantially safer than working with other forms of cabling. Copper cabling always poses the risk of carrying high voltages that would be dangerous to technicians and others. Optical cabling does not pose such risks.

- **Enhanced security**—Tapping optical fibers is possible, but difficult, and if accomplished results in additional loss, which is easily detectable. By contrast, since electrical cables radiate their signals, they are easier to tap unobtrusively.

HIGH FIBER DIET

IN AN EFFORT TO INCREASE HIS HEALTH
AND NETWORKING IQ, FRANK DISCOVERS
THE PERFECT ANTIDOTE

With that said, fiber isn't without its problems. One of the biggest, which has little do with the fiber per se, is the cost of components. While optic cabling may compare favorably with copper, optic devices are significantly more expensive than their electrical counterparts. On top of the cost issue though, providers need to grapple with two major fiber issues—installation problems and problems from bending of the fiber.

- **Installation problems**—Joining optical cables has never been particularly easy—if installers wanted to do the installation right, that is. When fiber optics were first introduced, the connectors allowing cables to be plugged and unplugged were unreliable, causing as much as 3 dB signal loss per connector (we'll get to more signal loss later). To avoid losing that much of the signal, installers fused fiber ends together by melting the glass, a task that requires precision equipment and is not something to be done in the howling snow or freezing cold.

- **Bending cables**—Light propagates down a fiber by reflecting off its walls like light off a mirror. Reflection only works, though, at the proper angle. Normally this isn't a problem, and fibers can be bent. Tight bends, however, or impressions, in the fiber, called microbends, can move the angle of incidence beyond the critical angle, causing some light to pass out of the core of the fiber.

FIBER CONSTRUCTION ....

Cars need frames and so do fibers. Less than 10 percent of the actual fiber carries the photons that make optical communications possible. The rest of the cable supplies the strength and environment resistance the cable needs to survive life in a conduit.

Let's get down to specifics. Fibers used in public networks consist of five components—a glass or silica core, cladding, buffer, strength material, and jacket (see Figure 4.1).

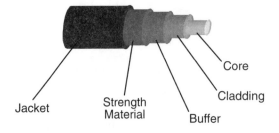

Figure 4.1
The five layers of a fiber optic cable.

NOT JUST ANY GLASS

Of course, when we speak about glass we're not talking the kind that's used in making bottles or windows. Household glass is a molten mixture of five components: sand or silicon dioxide (SiO_2); sodium carbonate (Na_2CO_3) to reduce the fusion temperature of the silica; calcium carbonate or limestone ($CaCO_3$); and magnesium carbonate ($MgCO_3$) to make the silica-sodium oxide mixture insoluble in water.

By contrast, the glass used in constructing fiber optic cabling is made from pure fused silicon dioxide with a few special ingredients. Without the addition of sodium carbonate, the silica in fiber optic cabling requires a very high temperature, 1700° Celsius, to fuse and form the glass.

The resulting glass delivers two qualities of interest to fiber manufacturers. There's a very high resistance to temperature (900°C for extended periods, 1200°C for short periods) and, since the fiber is pure silica, the rate of absorption of light is very low, enabling a signal to travel farther than would be possible using conventional glass.

Hold a fiber in your hand. What you're touching is the outer jacket. Fibers typically come encased in an orange jacket, though manufactures may use black or yellow. Sheaths are made from a range of material depending on the application. Polyvinyl chloride sheaths are common on fibers inside buildings. Polyethylene is prominent among outdoor cables and protects against environment challenges in under- and aboveground installations.

Peel away the outer jacket and you'll find the strength materials that protect the fiber from crushing or excessive tension during installation. Different strength materials can be used, including Aramid (better known as Kevlar), fiberglass yarn, and glass-reinforced plastic rods.

Inside the strength materials is a plastic coating. It's applied during the final step in the manufacturing process and protects the core and cladding from excessive bends, scratches, and dust. The coating is typically 250 to 900 microns (μm) thick and consists of two layers. Surrounding the cladding is a soft inner layer that cushions the fiber. The inner layer enables the fiber to be stripped mechanically, while the harder outer layer protects the fiber when being handled, particularly during installation and termination.

The core and the cladding of the fiber cable might be called the heart of the optical system. About the width of a human hair with the strength of steel, the core is made from silica and carries the light within the cable. The cladding wraps around the core, acting as a kind of supermirror, using the principle of total reflection to enable signals to propagate down the fiber—assuming they strike the fiber at the correct angle. The dimensions of the two are written as core size/cladding size

The core size is a major factor in determining how easily, and how much, light can be captured by the fiber. When an LED or laser injects light into the fiber, only that light is carried down the fiber that strikes the core at a particular angle, the acceptance angle, measured in terms of the **numerical aperture (NA)**. The larger the core, the easier it is to align the LED or laser.

**Dr. Geek on...
the Numerical
Aperture (NA)**

Unless light is injected into a fiber at the correct angle, it won't propagate down the fiber, but what is that angle? Fiber manufacturers speak about the Numerical Aperture as the measure of the angle size. The exact values can be calculated from the following formula:

$$\sqrt{RI_1^2 - RI_2^2}$$

where RI_1 is the refractive index of the core and the RI_2 is the refractive index of the cladding. To put this in another way, imagine that the fiber has a kind of cone at the edge indicating the size of the acceptance angle. The NA then is the sine of the largest angle within the cone of acceptance (see Figure 4.2).

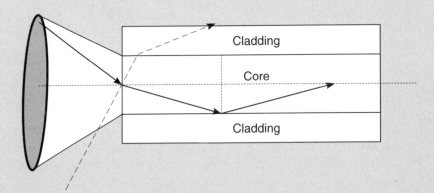

Figure 4.2
Rays that enter through the numerical aperture (NA) continue down the core; all others are lost into the cladding.

FIBER TYPES ....

The name of the game in optics is to carry a signal further without losing the clarity of the light pulse. The challenge, however, is twofold. First, a number of factors in the fiber attenuate or distort the signal as it travels down the fiber. Second, high-quality components needed to connect to smaller, better-performing fiber are costly. These problems led to the emergence of two main types of optical cables, multimode and single-mode fiber, and several subtypes. Each is governed by different standards stipulating a range of variables (see the Appendix for more information).

Within corporate networks, primarily **multimode fiber** is used. This fiber contains a relatively large core (50 or 62.5 μm) and can be used to distances up to around a kilometer. The larger core enables the pulse to travel down multiple paths, or modes, down the fiber (see Figure 4.3). There are two types of multimode fibers—step index and graded index. **Step index fiber** keeps the same refractive index (RI) across the core's diameter and is rarely used today. **Graded index (GI) fiber** gets a significantly longer reach by gradually increasing the RI across the core's diameter, reaching a high-point in the middle of the fiber and then gradually decreasing toward the cable perimeter (see Figure 4.4).

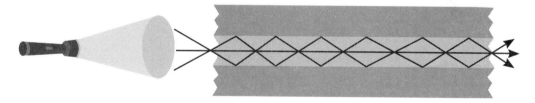

Figure 4.3
The wide core of a multimode fiber enables multiple light paths, called modes, to travel down the fiber.

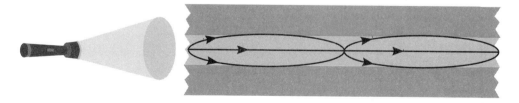

Figure 4.4
Unlike step index fiber, graded index fiber has a higher refractive index (RI) at the core, enabling rays from the modes to arrive at the destination simultaneously.

Dr. Geek on... the Cutoff Wavelength

Optical fibers become single moded at a particular wavelength, called the cut-off wavelength. Waves of lengths shorter than the cutoff wavelength will result in multimode transmission. To determine the point where fiber becomes single moded, use the following equation:

$$\lambda = \frac{\pi D \sqrt{n_0^2 - n_1^2}}{2.4}$$

where:

λ is lambda, the symbol for a wave

D is the diameter of the fiber

N_0 is the RI for the core

N_1 is the RI for the cladding

So suppose a fiber had an 8 micron core, the RI is 1.485 for the cladding and 0.5 for the core; then the formula would be:

$$\lambda = \frac{\pi 8 \times 10^3 \sqrt{1.5^2 - 1.485^2}}{2.4}$$

giving a cutoff wavelength of 1,281 nanometers. Any wave shorter than 1,281 nanometers on this cable will result in multimode transmission.

Within the public network, single-mode fibers are used. These fibers use much smaller cores (6–8 µm) to limit the number of modes at particular wavelengths and so they get much further reach, up to around 50 kilometers.

When the core is narrowed, part of the pulse's energy propagates down the cladding as well the fiber's core. This makes it misleading to speak of core diameter when it comes to single-mode fiber. Instead, fiber optic manufacturers speak of mode field diameter, a measurement encompassing the single mode's fiber core as well as the part of the cladding where performance drops off. Since this is not an exact point, mode field diameters can vary between manufacturers. At 1550 nm a typical mode field diameter will run around 9.2 to 10 µm.

There are two broad types of single-mode fibers—**non-dispersion shifted (NDSF)** and **dispersion shifted (DSF)**. NDSF fiber or standard single-mode fibers have a stepped index core to reach the longer distances. DSF fibers alter the fiber characteristics to take advantage of certain lower-attenuation characteristics of the fiber. **Zero-dispersion-shifted fiber (ZDSF)** alters the RI in such a way as to eliminate dispersion from the signal. **Nonzero-dispersion-shifted fiber (NZDSF)** introduces a nominal amount of dispersion to enable the fiber to work with the **dense wave-division**

multiplexing (DWDM) system and with the best amplifiers, **erbium-doped fiber amplifiers (EDFAs)**.

Special single-mode fibers have also been developed to compensate for specific dispersion problems that arise in single-mode fibers. **Dispersion-limiting fibers** are used to combat chromatic dispersion. **Polarization fiber** alters the RI to compensate for another dispersion problem called polarization mode dispersion (PMD). We'll learn more about PMD later in the chapter.

BEHIND THE TRANSMISSION BANDS.......................

Now we can understand the significance behind the transmission band model that we introduced in Chapter 3. First, the longer the wavelength, the less the signal weakens over the course of a cable run. Other things being equal, network operators prefer operating at higher windows because they can get longer distances. Of course there's a balance here. Operating at higher windows increases the cost and complexity of equipment.

As you get into the higher transmission windows, dispersion, or the spreading out of a pulse of light over long distances, becomes a major problem. Fiber manufacturers combat dispersion by optimizing the fiber for a particular wavelength, typically indicated by the zero-dispersion point (we'll learn more about the problems of dispersion and attenuation later in the chapter).

Multimode fibers operate in the first and second transmission windows, step-index fibers operate at 850 nm, and GI fibers operate at 850 and 1300 nm. Single-mode fibers operate at longer wavelengths, while standard single-mode fibers, or NDSF, have their zero-dispersion point at 1310 nm and ZDSF at 1550 nm.

Ironically, as we'll see, a little bit of dispersion can be a necessary ingredient for DWDM. Since DWDM operates at 1550, ZDSF can't be used, so NZDSF was developed, which moves the zero-dispersion point above 1550.

Those classic definitions, however, are starting to change as manufacturers develop fibers that can operate effectively at multiple wavelengths. This is particularly true with NZDSF cables. Lucent's Metrowave cable, for example, can work equally well at 1310 and 1550 nm, while its All Wave fibers work anywhere from 1310 to 1550 nm.

New fibers are also starting to work in the attenuation "hump" that occurs at around 1400 nm. The increase is due to Rayleigh scattering, caused by impurities stemming from the manufacturing process. Improvements in fiber manufacturing have reduced and, in some cases, eliminated this attenuation jump.

TRANSMISSION PROBLEMS ....

At each of these different wavelengths there are specifics characteristics and factors that complicate optical transmission. These factors fall into two broad groups—linear effects and nonlinear effects. Linear effects increase in proportion to the length of the cable. The major linear effects are attenuation and dispersion. Nonlinear effects change in proportion to the signal's power, not the distance covered. They become increasingly important and limiting as networks operate at higher speeds. Common nonlinear effects cover scattering and four-wave mixing.

Linear Effects

By far the most common linear effect is attenuation—the weakening of the signal as it propagates down a fiber. To understand the importance of attenuation in fiber's development, look back at Figure 3.9. Notice that attenuation levels are very high in the first transmission band and substantially lower in the higher bands. This shift led fiber manufacturers to look beyond multimode fiber for a means to transmit at higher levels.

The high attenuation at the lower levels is due primarily to a phenomenon called Rayleigh scattering (after the British physicist Lord Rayleigh) and, to a lesser extent, to absorption. Both are measured in terms of decibels.

When photons collide with atoms, additional photons are released, causing light. Two other effects also occur. Some of the light energy is absorbed and some of the light is scattered (see Figure 4.5).

As light encounters particles that are smaller in diameter than its own wavelength, the particles direct some of the light in another direction. This effect occurs in optical fibers because of minute variations in the density of the glass that arise during the cooling process.

Scattering is a bigger problem at shorter wavelengths than at longer ones. This is because Rayleigh scattering is a function of the relative size of the scattering subject to the wavelength, which is why optical communications are limited to wavelengths over 800 nm. At shorter wavelengths, scattering prevents effective communications.

Scattering isn't the only phenomenon that occurs. Our ability to see color results from the second phenomenon, the absorption and, by extension, the reflection of light by an object. How much light is absorbed depends on the particular substance and the wavelength of the light. Ordinary glass absorbs comparatively little light and so it appears to be transparent. A key development in producing the highly refined silica of fibers was the removal of certain impurities that cause higher absorption rates.

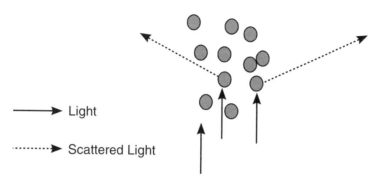

→ Light

┈┈┈► Scattered Light

Figure 4.5
Rayleigh scattering.

All objects absorb light, but how can we calculate that absorption rate? If only absorption affects the light, then use the following equation:

$$(1 - \alpha)^D$$

**Dr. Geek on...
an Object's
Absorption
Rate**

where:

    α is alpha, the symbol for the fraction of light absorbed per unit length

    D is the length of the fiber.

    So if a fiber had a 0.5% absorption rate per cm, the amount of light remaining after 1 meter (100 centimeters) would be:

$$(1 - .005)^{100} = 61\%$$

DECIBELS—WHAT DO THEY MEAN? ....

The cumulative effect of absorption and scattering is the total loss, or attenuation, and is expressed in decibels. Decibels (abbreviated dB) are peculiar units because the magnitude of the impact is understated. A 5 dB loss means that just a little more than 32 percent of the original power remains, and a 10 dB loss leaves just 10 percent of the original power (see Table 4.1).

Table 4.1 Sample Values for Decibel Loss[*]

Loss in Decibels	Percent of Input Power Remaining
0.1	98%
0.5	89%
1	79%
2	63%
5	32%
10	10%
20	1%
50	0%

[*] *Calculated with the following formula: power remaining = $10^{(-dB/10)}$*

So why bother with decibels at all? The reason is that, without them, attenuation calculations would be much more complicated. With decibels you just add up the attenuations for the total loss.

At times, manufacturers talk about decibels relative to some specific level, namely 1 milliwatt (1 mW or dBm) or 1 microwatt (1 μW or dBμ). Above these levels the amount of loss is positive; below them, it negative (see Table 4.2)

Table 4.2 Sample Decibel to Milliwatt and Microwatt Conversions

dBm	mW	μW
0.1	-10	100
0.5	-3	500
1	0	1,000
2	3	2,000
3	5	5,000
9	10	100,000

DISPERSION ....

The other major linear factor impacting single-mode and multimode fibers is **dispersion**, the spreading out of a light pulse as it travels down the fiber. The phenomenon occurs because the speed of a light pulse through a fiber depends on the wavelength and the particular mode used. Since modes are of slightly varying wavelengths and because a pulse consists of multiple wavelengths over long distances, light pulses spread out. There are four major types of dispersion, derived from multimode transmission, the dependence of RI on wavelength, variations in fiber properties based on wavelength, and the two different polarizations in single-mode fibers.

Modal Dispersion

The large core in multimode fibers allows a pulse of light to take several paths, or modes, through the fiber. Using Maxwell's equations, named after the British physicist James Clerk Maxwell (1831–1879), engineers can show a number of modes through a multimode cable, ranging up to several hundred. Some will go through the center of the cable, others out toward the edge, and still others may be elliptical in form, never traversing the center of the core at any one time. Because of their varying paths, modes end up with different lengths.

The most immediate impact of so many modes of different lengths is to limit distances to about a kilometer. Longer distances aren't possible because of **modal dispersion**. Since modes aren't the same length, light pulses reach the receiver faster on shorter modes than on longer ones. So they might, for example, be transmitted every 2 ns but disperse or spread out to say every 10 ns at the end of the signal, making the light pulse unreadable over longer runs.

Dr. Geek on... the Modal Dispersion

We've learned about modal dispersion, but how do engineers calculate the amount of modal dispersion over a given link? The formula is a comparatively easy one:

$$\Delta t = \text{dispersion (ns/km)} \times \text{distance (km)}$$

where:

Δt (pronounced "delta t") represents total pulse spreading

dispersion (ns/km) is the amount of dispersion in a link expressed in terms of nanoseconds per kilometer (ns/km)

distance (km) is the length of the fiber run in kilometers.

So if a fiber run were 100 kilometers with a dispersion of rate of 8 ns/km, then the total amount of dispersion would be 800 ns.

This is why the RI changes on a GI fiber. Think of it as increasing the resistance on the shorter modes, those closer to the center of the core, enabling all of the waves to arrive at about the same time. Of course, developing these ideal RI gradients is never easy, making it very difficult to totally eliminate modal dispersion.

Under ideal circumstances modes remain independent, or orthogonal, of one another. However, any number of factors in the construction of the fiber system can change this phenomenon and cause the energy pulse to jump, or couple, from one mode to another. When connectors are misaligned, some modes will receive the power originally meant for other modes. Similarly, when two fibers are fused or connected together, a difference in RIs may cause power to jump to the wrong modes. Microbends are another problem. Minute bends in the fiber's surface due to stresses applied to the fiber can change the angle of incidence experienced by the light pulse, causing the power to escape the fiber and jump between modes.

The effect of this phenomenon, called mode coupling, is mixed. On one hand, it has a statistical effect that can counteract modal dispersion. Given a sufficient number of modes, the differences in pulse velocities will likely decrease, improving the quality of the signal.

On the other hand, when used with high-quality lasers, mode coupling leads to modal noise. The light sources used in long-distance communications generate a very narrow band of light. When this light launches into the multimode cable, the modes end up carrying light of the same wavelength and in phase. After a short distance the signals will be out of phase with one another. When the power jumps from one mode to the next, the waves collide, likely resulting in destructive interference and a loss of power. If the laser changes wavelength even slightly, then when the modes couple, the amplitude of the mixed signal will also change rather abruptly. When this fluctuating signal meets an irregularity in the fiber, power is lost in random amounts, resulting in noise and significant deterioration in signal power.

Chromatic Dispersion

As standard single-mode fibers, NDSFs were attractive because they avoided the modal dispersion and attenuation problems of the multimode fibers. However, NDSFs have their own problem of chromatic dispersion, a combination of material and waveguide dispersion.

Linguists will note that the word chromatic has to do with or pertains to color. Understanding that, you might guess that chromatic dispersion has to do with the spreading out or dispersing of color. You wouldn't be far off. Any light pulse, no matter how precise the laser, contains a range of wavelengths at different frequencies or what in the visible spectrum would be called different colors. Those rays will propagate down the fiber at different velocities, since the resistance referred to as the RI varies in accordance with the wavelength. The longer the wave, the higher the RI. The upshot is that the wave will spread out as the signal travels down the wire. Spread it out enough and the signal becomes unintelligible.

At the same time, the velocity of these wavelengths is also affected by waveguide dispersion. Here again one might guess that waveguide dispersion is a distortion of the pulse from factors related to the waveguide—in this case, the fiber. Not a bad guess at all. More specifically, as waves move down the fiber, the light's electromagnetic fields extend into the cladding. The longer the wavelength, the more these fields overlap with the cladding.

Keep in mind that the core's RI tends to be higher than that of the cladding. The impact of the RI varies in accordance with the length of the wave. Since longer waves travel more in the cladding than shorter waves, the longer waves see a smaller RI and end up traveling faster.

The two factors, material and waveguide dispersion, cancel each other out a particular wavelength. And that wavelength is—you guessed it—1310 nanometers. Stick to that wavelength, and dispersion is minimized.

**Dr. Geek on...
Calculating
Total
Dispersion**

Chromatic dispersion is a major challenge for single-mode fibers, but how can we calculate how much of a hit results from the phenomenon, and how does chromatic dispersion combine with other forms of dispersion? Chromatic dispersion is the sum of waveguide and material dispersion. It can also be calculated if a single number for dispersion is provided per kilometer using the following equation:

$\Delta t_{chromatic}$ = dispersion (ps/nm/km) × distance (km) × spectral width (nm)

where:

$\Delta t_{chromatic}$ (pronounced "delta t") is the total amount of chromatic dispersion in the link

dispersion (ps/nm/km) is the amount of dispersion in picoseconds (ps) per nanometer (nm) per kilometer (km)

distance is the length of the link in kilometers

spectral width is the width of the pulse in nm.

So for a system operating at 1500 nm, where dispersion is 17 ps/nm/km over 100 kilometers, with a laser whose spectral width is 6 nm, the total amount of chromatic dispersion would be 173,400ps.

Once chromatic dispersion is determined, then figure out the total dispersion for the link using the following equation:

$$\Delta t_{\text{total}} = \sqrt{(\Delta t_{\text{modal}})^2 + (\Delta\lambda\Delta t_{\text{chromatic}})^2}$$

$\Delta t_{\text{total}}=$

where:

Δt_{total} is the total amount of dispersion

Δt_{modal} is the total amount of modal dispersion

$\Delta\lambda$ is the range of wavelengths of the pulse

$\Delta t_{\text{chromatic}}$ is the total amount of chromatic dispersion

Polarization-Mode Dispersion

Normally, the two modes in a single-mode fiber don't interfere with one another and so we speak only of a single mode. Yet, with any rule there must be an exception. Under the right conditions, namely speeds over 2.5 Gbits/s, the time differential between the polarizations becomes so great that the pulse becomes elongated or smudged. This problem, called polarization-mode dispersion, is actually more complicated, of course, resulting not only from the sheer speeds, but also from random factors arising from stresses inside and outside the fiber.

**Dr. Geek on...
PMD**

Polarization-mode dispersion (PMD) is the only type of modal dispersion that poses a serious problem for single-mode fiber and even then only on very high speed links. Calculating the total dispersion on a single-mode fiber with PMD is very similar to dispersion calculations on a multimode fiber. Just replace total modal dispersion for the total PMD dispersion and you get:

$$\Delta t_{\text{total}} = \sqrt{(\Delta t_{\text{polarizationmode}})^2 + (\Delta\lambda\Delta t_{\text{chromatic}})^2}$$

where:

Δt_{total} is the total amount of dispersion

$\Delta t_{\text{polarization mode I}}$ is the total amount of PMD

$\Delta\lambda$ is the range of wavelengths of the pulse

D + $t_{\text{chromatic}}$ is the total amount of chromatic dispersion

Nonlinear Effects

Aside from linear effects, like attenuation and dispersion, there are nonlinear effects that increase in proportion not to the length of fiber, but to the intensity of a signal. Since these effects depend on the amount of power passing through a unit area, they are more likely to be found in single-mode fibers with their 8 μm cores than in multi-mode fibers with a 52 or 62.5 μm core.

Brillouin and Raman Scattering

Rayleigh isn't the only form of scattering that network designers face. Two other types, Brillouin and Raman, also impact network transmission, albeit in a nonlinear fashion.

With Brillouin scattering, attenuation is increased at the transmitter through the effect of acoustic waves. Here's what happens. When signal power reaches a certain point, it starts to generate acoustic vibrations. Those vibrations change the core's density and by extension its refractive index (RI). The changes in the RI can cause the light to scatter, generating more acoustic waves.

Ultimately, this effect sends a light wave slightly shifted in frequency back toward the light source, creating attenuation on the link. The shorter the pulse length, the more power required to cause Brillouin scattering and thus the lower the likelihood of the effect occurring at high data rates. By preventing the optical signal from traveling back to the light source and keeping power levels in range on narrow-linewidth laser sources, the Brillouin scattering effect can be prevented.

Raman scattering is different. Sometimes light waves can absorb additional energy from atoms. More specifically, when light strikes an atom that's vibrating, the light can absorb an amount of energy equivalent to the atom's vibration. The result is not only a scattering of the light, but also a changing of the light's wavelength.

More laser power is required to cause Raman scattering than Brillouin scattering. When the Raman scattering does occur, crosstalk between two waves in the fiber can be the result. By picking the right wavelengths, the effect of Raman scattering can be reduced. However, it does limit fiber runs with many amplifiers, and its effects are felt more on shorter waves than longer ones.

Four-Wave Mixing

As providers started moving to EDFAs and DWDM gear, another phenomenon, four-wave mixing, gained attention and eventually led to the demise of ZDF in the public network. Both EDFAs and DWDM gear operate in the third transmission windows. EDFAs boost the signal without regard to noise or other interference, and DWDM equipment divides the link up into small channels separated by a fixed amount of bandwidth. Data is sent over each of these subchannels, increasing the performance of the link.

The problem is that two or three signals can combine to create a third or fourth wave (hence the name). Where channels are separated by equal frequency increments, this new wave causes crosstalk by landing on top of an existing channel. If spacing is not equal, four-wave mixing produces noise between channels.

Ironically, the problem can be prevented through chromatic dispersion. The lasers used in single-mode transmission produce coherent light, where the signals are in phase with one another. So when these signals travel down the fiber and eventually combine, they form a new wave. Dispersion counteracts this effect by ensuring that signals do not stay in phase with each other for very long. ZDFs exacerbated this problem because they eliminated dispersion from the band where DWDM and EDFAs functioned. NZDFs evolved precisely because of this problem and allowed a moderate amount of dispersion to occur in the fiber.

SHORT CUTS...

Fibers are constructed from five major components—the jacket, strength material, coating, cladding and core.

Light travels through the core bouncing off the cladding, using the principle of total internal reflection. This works only because the core contains a higher refractive index (RI) than the cladding.

There are two major types of fiber, multimode and single mode. Multimode has a relatively large core, enabling multiple modes or paths for light to travel down through the fiber. Single-mode fiber has a much smaller core and thus there is only one effective path or mode through it.

Multimode's ability to gather light is measured through the numerical aperture; single mode's primarily through the mode field diameter.

There are two types of multimode fibers, stepped index and graded index. They differ in how light propagates down through the different modes. Stepped-index fiber has a uniform RI across all modes, so on long fiber runs light on the shorter modes reaches the receiver significantly earlier than on the longer modes. Graded-index fiber changes the RI on the way across the modes such that light on the longer modes arrives at the receiver at nearly the same time as light on the shorter modes.

There are two broad types of single-mode fibers—non-dispersion shifted (NDSF) and dispersion shifted (DSF). NDSF fibers or standard single-mode fibers have a stepped index core to reach the longer distances. DSF fibers alter the characteristics of the fiber to combat pulse dispersion. Zero-dispersion-shifted fibers (ZDSF) alter the RI in such a way as to eliminate dispersion from the signal, but they can't work with DWDM or EDFAs. Non-zero-dispersion-shifted fibers (NZDSF) introduce a nominal amount of dispersion in order to work with the DWDM and EDFAs.

There are seven transmission windows. Multimode fiber uses only the first two at around 850 and 1300 nm. NDSF uses the second window at 1310 m. ZDSF uses the fifth window at 1550 but can't work with DWDM. NZDSF cables use different windows. They all can use the fifth window and work with DWDM gear, with some also using the second, third, sixth, and seventh windows.

There are two major types of transmission effects. Linear effects, namely attenuation and dispersion, increase in proportion to the length of the cable. Nonlinear effects, like Brillouin and Raman scattering or four-wave mixing, change in proportion to the signal's power, not the distance covered.

5 Optical Components

In this chapter...

There's more to fiber optic network than just fiber. Simple networks need light sources to generate the light that will travel down the fiber, and they need detectors to receive those signals. Most networks are far more complicated than that and need a variety of equipment to send and receive, boost, mix, match, sort, and clean light signals before, after, and during their journey down fibers.

Over long distances, keeping the signal sharp is imperative, and that's why providers use amplifiers and regenerators. Couplers let us join fibers together, and interferometers are useful in measuring the amount of light on a surface. The alphabet soup grows even thicker with isolators, circulators, filters, and gratings. We'll look at all of these in clarifying the low-level workings of today's optical networks.

SEMICONDUCTORS..

Most optical components fall into the category of semiconductors—those peculiar materials sitting somewhere between conductors, like metal, that conduct electricity, and insulators, like glass and plastic, that do not. Conductivities of **semiconductors** are a tiny fraction (a millionth or so) of those of metals but much higher than those of insulators.

The difference has to do with the outer electrons and how closely they are tied to the atom. In metals, the outer electrons of each atom are delocalized. They are free to move throughout the material, thereby giving metals their high conductivities, and by vibrating when hit by light waves, giving metals their typically shiny appearances (see Figure 5.1). In insulators, however, the outer electrons are trapped closely to the individual pairs of atoms; they are not free to move and so cannot conduct electricity (see Figure 5.2).

Figure 5.1
In metals, the atoms are arranged in regular structures called crystals and are surrounded by electron clouds that are free to move.

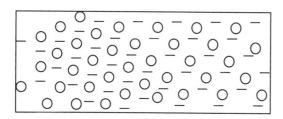

Figure 5.2
With insulators, electrons are bound to an atom within the material. The charges cannot move in response to an applied electrical field.

Semiconductors, on the other hand, are crystalline materials that have conductivities somewhere between those of metals and insulators. The outer electrons are localized, but some of them—the exact number depending on the energy within the material—are delocalized. They have sufficient energy to leave their association with particular atoms and move through the crystal structure, leaving an energy deficiency, called a hole, in the atom, which gives it a positive charge (see Figure 5.3).

What's useful here is that a semiconductor can be given an electrical charge by introducing impurities—a process called doping. **N-doped** semiconductors are materials to which elements have been added such as nitrogen, which, after bonding with silicon, contains an extra electron in its outermost shell, giving the combination a negative charge. **P-doped** semiconductors, on the other hand, are doped with elements such as boron. After bonding with silicon, boron is left with a hole, giving the material a positive charge.

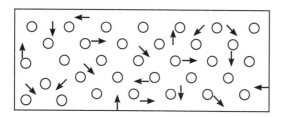

Figure 5.3
Semiconductors are somewhere between conductors and insulators. Some electrons are free to move within the crystal, so if an electrical field is applied, most of the electrons move away from it.

Light Sources

By connecting these two materials—p-doped and n-doped semiconductors—into what's called a p-n junction we form a diode, the basis for the **light emitting diodes (LEDs)** used in the local communications and the **lasers** (Light Amplification by the Stimulated Emission of Radiation) used in the optical networks of the public networks.

Let's take a closer look. When a voltage is passed across a p-n junction, the holes of the p-doped and the electrons of the n-doped semiconductors flow toward the junction and combine. The electrons fall to a lower energy state, giving off the energy that we call light in a process called **spontaneous emission** (see Figure 5.4).

The exact wavelength of the light depends on the specific materials used. Gallium arsenide (GaAs) LEDs, for example, emit waves of red light (620–700 nm), while gallium phosphide (GaP) emits a greenish color (around 500 to 578 nm). By mixing different proportions of indium and gallium, we can produce light of the different wavelengths used for optical communications. Indium gallium arsenide (InGaAs) emits light near infrared at 1300 nm. Indium gallium arsenide phosphide (InGaAsP) produces longer waves up to 1700 nm. The light is then tuned to specific wavelengths by using heterojunctions—junctions composed of substantially different materials (see Figure 5.5).

Lasers, on the other hand, prevent spontaneous emissions from occurring by positioning a semireflective layer (about 70 percent reflective) at each end of the junction, forming what's called the laser cavity. Now, when the electrons are brought to their higher energy state, the resulting photons can't escape and keep on bumping into the other atoms in the laser cavity, releasing more photons in a process called **stimulated emission**. All the while voltage continues to travel across the p-n junction, causing the electrons and holes to combine, releasing more photons.

Switching to the wave concept of light for a moment, only frequencies that can resonate in this cavity are built up. All others get attenuated. This means that the photons are identical.

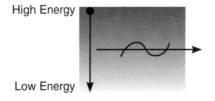

Figure 5.4
When an electron falls from a higher to a lower energy state, the lost energy is emitted as a photon and a wave.

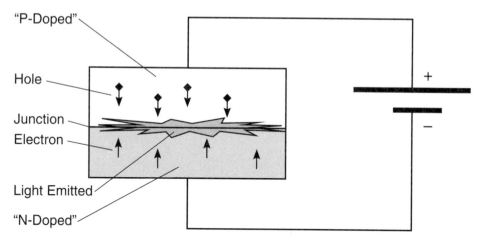

Figure 5.5
LEDs are largely a junction between P-doped and N-doped semiconductors.
When a voltage is applied across the semiconductors, the electrons and holes
flow toward a junction, where they combine, releasing energy as light.

At some point a state called population inversion is reached, where there are
more atoms in an excited state than in the ground state. At that point, the photons can
travel through the semireflective layer, emitting an intense, nearly monochromatic, coherent beam of light, or a beam of light where the waves are in phase.

While effective over short distances and fairly inexpensive, LEDs have a number of shortcomings that preclude their use in the public network. The light emitted by
the stimulated p-n junction consists of a wider range of wavelengths than that emitted
by lasers. This limits the distance from the transmitter at which the signal may still be
read, as modal results in individual signal bits smearing into each other and becomes a
major problem over long distances. What's more, LEDs emit diffuse light, so the signal becomes attenuated in a shorter distance than the light emitted by lasers, which is
coherent.

The Laser Family

The mode of operation we've just described is for the common Fabry Perot laser.
There are numerous other lasers, which we can categorize according to a number of
criteria. We'll use two: the direction from which light escapes the laser cavity, and the
operating wavelength.

Most lasers today emit light from the side, as we've described. These lasers are
called **edge emitters** and include Fabry Perot lasers as well as the **Distributed Feed-**

back Lasers (DFLs), Distributed Bragg Reflector (DBR) lasers, **neodymium lasers**, and **fiber lasers**.

Fabry-Perot lasers aren't entirely monochromatic. The signal includes a range of wavelengths. A more precise beam is available from DFLs, which add a kind of corrugated grating to the Fabry-Perot design (see Figure 5.6). The grating is spread, or distributed, across the upper part of the entire cavity between the semiconductor surfaces and only allows the undesired frequencies through. The net result is that only light of the desired frequency builds up in the lasing cavity, creating a highly monochromatic beam of light. **DBR lasers** work in a similar way, except that the grating is placed outside the lasing cavity. The bad news? The additional design complexity can make the more precise laser hundreds of times more expensive than a Fabry-Perot laser.

Where a powerful laser is required, such as for crossing the Atlantic, neodymium lasers are used. Here a cavity is made out of a higher-powered material, such as YAG (yttrium aluminum garnet) or YLF (yttrium lithium fluoride), doped with neodymium and enclosed between the two mirrors. The solid cavity material is excited by an external light source, rather than by electronic energy, producing a high-intensity beam of light.

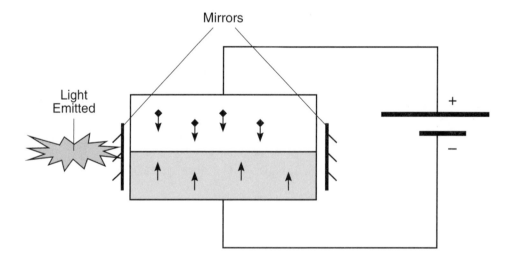

Figure 5.6
Fabry lasers add a pair of semireflective layers (mirrors) to the LED. When photons are released, they bounce back and forth within the cavity (the space between the mirrors). An intense, coherent light beam is emitted. Photons of inappropriate wavelength are attenuated, so the beam of light emitted has a narrow bandwidth.

A similar concept is used in fiber lasers, where a length of regular silica fiber is doped with erbium and placed between two semireflective layers. When energy is supplied by pumping in light of a low wavelength, the erbium ions emit photons of light having a wavelength of 1550 nm. The mirrors cause the light to lase, and an intense beam of coherent light is produced, having a wavelength of 1550 nm, which is ideal for long-distance transmission. Erbium-doped fibers are also used as amplifiers, as we'll see later.

VCSELs

Lasers in the second category, vertical cavity surface-emitting semiconductor lasers (VCSELs), emit laser light in the direction of the electrodes—that is, through the top—hence the word "vertical" in the name. Like other semiconductor lasers, VCSELs are essentially p-n junctions. As current flows towards the p-n junction, holes and electrons combine, emitting photons. Here the "mirrors" are multiple layers of semitransparent materials whose number, thickness, and materials determine the wavelength of the laser beam emitted (see Figure 5.7).

VCSELs have a couple of benefits over edge emitters. They're much easier to manufacture. Edge emitters need to be cut from their material, packaged, and then tested. VCSELs can be tested while they are on the wafer on which they're developed. If

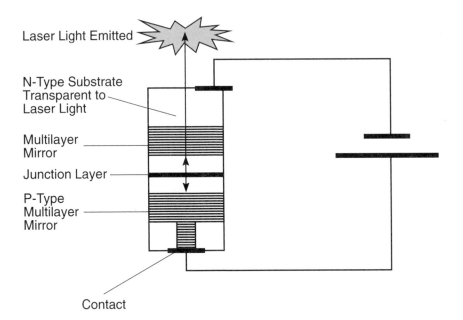

Figure 5.7
A vertical-cavity surface-emitting laser.

there's a problem, the high cost of packaging is avoided. VCSELs are also more efficient and consume less power than edge-emitting lasers. They produce less heat, requiring less dissipation, and generally last longer. Finally, like other laser types, VCSELS can be modulated at high speed, so they can generate signals faster than 1 gigabit/second.

Currently available VCSELs are made of GaAs (gallium arsenide), and emit light having wavelengths from about 750 to 1000 nm. These wavelengths are not long enough to be transmitted very far down a fiber, and so VCSELs are not used much for long-distance communication, but are used for LANs within a single building or a university campus and the like, where lots of information is shared over short distances.

Tuning In

Most lasers today can operate on only a single frequency or wavelength. There are tunable lasers that can adjust the emitted wavelength of the released light. While regular lasers have fixed cavity size and refractive index (RI), yielding a beam of light of a fixed frequency range, tunable lasers can adjust their cavity's characteristics to create light of selectable frequencies. How they adjust the characteristics of their light cavity depends on the implementation.

One approach is to physically increase and decrease the cavity walls. That's the idea of external cavity lasers. However, their complexity typically renders them more suitable for the lab than the field.

A more practical way of achieving the same result is to use a piezoelectric material. Piezoelectrics convert pressure into voltage and vice versa. By applying a voltage to a piezoelectric material, a mechanical stress is formed, changing the dimensions of the material and generally the refractive index as well.

Modulation

In order for signals to carry information, they need to be modulated. Today's optical systems use a very simple kind of modulation, on-off keying, where the signal is present (a one) or not (a zero). The challenge is in making this transition fast enough at extremely high data rates.

With **direct modulation**, the light source can be turned on and off by changing the current passing through it. At high speed, five problems are associated with this approach:

- The amount of output power that a laser can generate is limited, restricting spacing between amplifiers.

- Modulation speed also becomes limited, which restricts the capacity of the network.

- Direct modulation lowers the possible extinction ratio, or the difference between the light signal at full power (a 1 bit) and at low power (a zero bit), which in turn reduces the allowable distance between a receiver and a transmitter.

- Nonlinearities arise that can distort the analog signals used in cable TV networks.

- Finally, direct modulation increases wavelength chirp, adding to the kinds of dispersion problems we discussed in Chapter 4. Wavelength chirp is the rapid change in a laser's center wavelength produced by the change in the refractive index as the current driving the laser increases and decreases.

At rates over 1 Gbit/s providers use external modulators. Electro-optic modulators, for example, rely on the electro-optic effect to change the refractive index of certain materials by applying an electric field to them. Decreasing the RI speeds up the light; increasing the RI slows the light down.

These modulators split the light into two waveguides. If the light needs to be signaled ON, then voltage is applied equally to both channels. The two signal recombine, constructive interference occurs, and the light carries ON. If the signal needs to be turned OFF, then a voltage is applied such that the RI changes and one signal is 180 degrees out of phase with the other signal. When they meet, destructive interference occurs, the signals cancel each other out, and the signal is turned OFF. In reality this process is more complicated, using voltages of different polarities on each channel, but the basic effect remains the same.

DETECTORS

Lasers and LEDs emit light. **Detectors**... well... detect light. Light detectors sit in the receivers of optical gear, enabling the equipment to translate the optical signal back to an electrical one.

They do this by situating a semiconductive material facing the waveguide. The light pulse travels down the waveguide and strikes this material. The electrons that are loosely held in the outer shells of the atoms in the semiconductor are knocked free, creating an electrical current. The more radiation that's incident on the material, the greater the flow of electrical current (see Figure 5.8).

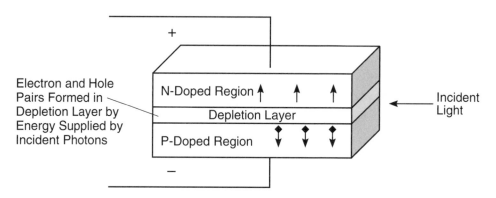

Electron and Hole
Pairs Formed in
Depletion Layer by
Energy Supplied by
Incident Photons

Figure 5.8
Principle of the photodetector.

Just how much current the detector generates depends on the material. If the light source is too faint, the receiver won't function. The spectral range that can be detected is also a function of the materials used in the detector. Silicon detects light in the range 400 to 1100 nm, gallium arsenide (GaAs) has a similar range (400 to 1000 nm). Germanium is useful at longer wavelengths (800 to about 1600 nm), and InGaAs and InGaAsP are particularly useful for detecting the near-infrared wavelengths used for telecommunications.

Two other detector characteristics are also important to consider. The response time of a detector is a measure of how quickly it can respond to variations in the input light intensity, which determines how fast the device can track incoming signals, or at what frequency the device will operate. Noise characteristics are critical. Often spurious signals are generated, due to temperature effects for example, by the detectors. This parameter is important for determining at what low levels of input light a particular device will still work adequately.

AMPLIFIERS ....

Signals fade over distance. That's a truism for optical just as for electrical communications. Naturally, the distances are much greater on optical networks, but the problems still exist.

To address those problems, three types of devices are used, **amplifiers**, **regenerators**, and **repeaters**. Optical amplifiers are all-optical devices that increase the intensity of a signal detected, noise and all. They typically do the first level of regeneration, amplification (see Figure 5.9). Regenerators are more sophisticated—detecting the optical signal, converting it into an electronic signal, cleaning it up, and retransmitting it as an optical signal again—and generally they use electronics. Repeaters fall somewhere be-

THE PHOTONIC HEALTH-SPA

tween all optical amplifiers and regenerators. Repeaters are also electro-optical devices, but, typically, they only provide amplification and reshaping, not full regeneration of a signal. Since the introduction of optical amplifiers, however, repeaters are rarely used.

Amplifiers are devices that enlarge and strengthen signals without distorting the original waveshape. A loudspeaker is an acoustical **amplifier**, and optical amplifiers perform similar functions for optical signals. Amplifiers help maintain the signal strength over long distances. Unfortunately they are nondiscriminatory and will amplify noise and distortion as well as the desired signal.

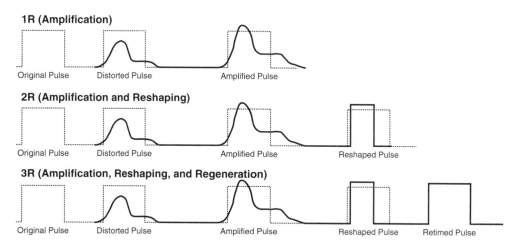

Figure 5.9
Amplification vs. regeneration.

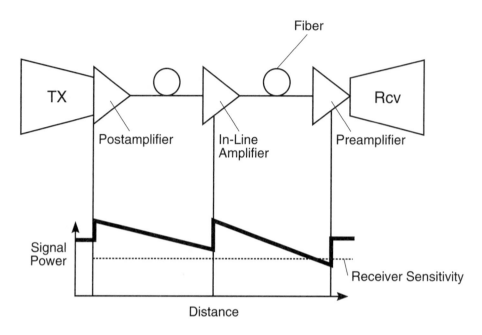

Figure 5.10
Amplification occurs in three locations in the network—after transmission (postamplification), during transmission (in-line amplification), and prior to re-ception (preamplification). Amplifiers are placed at points where signal power approaches receiver sensitivity.

There are three places in the network where amplifiers can be located. **Postam-plifiers** are placed directly after a transmitter to increase the strength of a signal be-fore transmission. **In-line amplifiers** sit every 80 to 100 km along an optical fiber link, to make up for signal attenuation. **Preamplifiers** are placed just before a receiver and magnify the signal to a power level within the receiver's sensitivity range (see Figure 5.10).

Exactly how amplifiers work depends on their construction. The most widely used amplifiers in current optical telecommunications are **Erbium-Doped Fiber Am-plifiers** (EDFAs). Erbium is a rare element that's added in small amounts to the fiber's silica core. As a weak, attenuated signal passes through an erbium-doped piece of fi-ber, light is added or pumped in at a second wavelength so as not to interfere with the signal. The erbium ions resonate in response to the light signal passing through the fi-ber, using extra energy taken from the added wavelength. The net result is that the er-bium ions amplify the signal, thereby increasing the distance to which the signal will travel (see Figure 5.11).

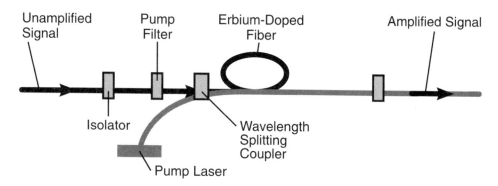

Figure 5.11
Structure of an erbium-doped fiber amplifier (EDFA).

Interjecting a pumped beam into the fiber could have an adverse effect, however. The light could travel back down the fiber to the laser, causing noise. An optical isolator is used to prevent this. Isolators enable light to flow in one direction down a fiber, but not in the reverse direction.

Perfect? Not exactly. Isolators will interfere with the forward flow of light, typically degrading the light signal by perhaps 2 dB. Some light will also flow in the reverse direction, but it will typically be 40 or 50 dB weaker than the input signal.

The big news with EDFAs, though, is that they are comparatively cheap, very efficient, and have high output powers with low noise and minimal crosstalk between adjacent fibers. If they have a drawback, it's that they are effective only with wavelengths around 1550 nm in the near infrared.

Lower frequencies can be boosted through by doping the fiber with another element, prasedymium, to form **Prasedymium-Doped Fiber Amplifiers** (**PDFAs**). These show promise for amplifying signals transmitted at 1300 nm. Simlarly, Raman amplifiers work effectively at 1300, 1400, and 1500 nm. They show promise for **dense wavelength division multiplexing (DWDM)** digital transmission systems.

Raman amplifiers use the Raman effect, discovered by the Indian physicist Sir Chandrasekhara Venkata Raman in 1928. As we mentioned in our discussion of Raman scattering in Chapter 3, the **Raman effect** is a change in frequency observed when light is scattered in a transparent material.

We can see this effect by looking at the effect on monochromatic light, such as that obtained from a laser, passing through a transparent gas, liquid, or solid. Without the interceding materials, the laser would produce a single color. However, when the light encounters the materials, the photons lose or gain energy by elastic collisions with the molecules of the transparent substance. A line of colors, called the **Raman**

spectrum, is produced from the longer and shorter wavelengths. This spectrum varies with the nature of the material that scatters the light.

Since the Raman gain spectrum is not locked to fixed energy levels as are rare-earth elements, such as erbium, Raman gain can be generated at any wavelength in the infrared, as long as the requisite pump light is available. This feature allows Raman amplification to be applied across the entire transmission window of silica optical fibers.

Amplifiers using the Raman effect are more costly than EDFAs due to the more powerful pump (roughly a watt) and long fiber lengths that are required. Nevertheless, they have the major advantage of providing optical gain throughout the low-loss fiber transmission window, so they can be used as a silica-based technology alternative to PDFAs or chalcogenide fiber amplifiers in the 1.3-μm window. Recent improvements in the "active" fiber design have yielded Raman power efficiencies as high as ~0.06 dB/mW in certain types of fiber, which, although small compared to the efficiencies reported for EDFAs (11 dB/mW), may offer a viable alternative at non-erbium wavelengths. Today, Raman Amplification is playing an important role in ultra-long haul systems that boost long-distance transmissions from about 500 kilometers between repeaters to 1500 or more kilometers between repeaters.

WAVE-DIVISION MULTIPLEXERS...............................

Boosting optical distances is the job of amplifiers. Extracting more capacity out of existing fibers is the job of wave-division multiplexers. By combining lasers together with a splash of filters and gratings, wave-division multiplexers can increase fiber's capacity a hundredfold.

Creating multiple pathways is critical because transmission systems at some point become bounded by the speed of light or the current state of electronics. By creating multiple parallel channels, higher performance can be reached without resorting to some kind of futuristic hyperdrive or the like.

As we saw back in Chapter 2, the idea of wave-division multiplexing (WDM) is to pack or multiplex wavelengths incoming on individual fibers into a single fiber. Often you'll hear about these wavelengths as different colors, though at this edge of the spectrum (typically in the 1500-nanometer range where attenuation is at a minimum) there isn't a difference in the color between the wavelengths.

In many ways WDM functions like a radio network. Each wavelength is used to carry data and is assigned a channel number, somewhat like different radio stations using different wavelengths to transmit different programs through the same airspace, except that instead of being broadcast over the airwaves, the information is narrowcast

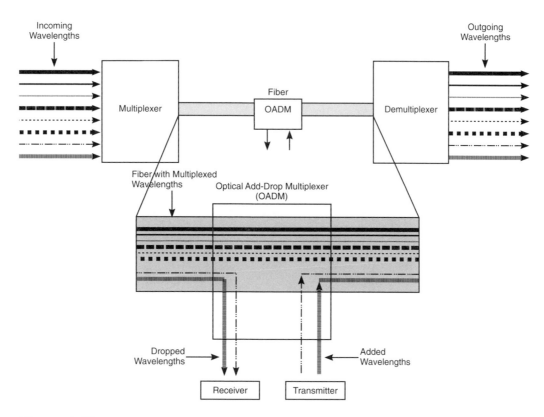

Figure 5.12
A WDM system.

down a fiber to a dedicated receiver, where it is extracted by a **demultiplexer**. Alternatively, an **optical add-drop multiplexer (OADM)** can extract a select range of wavelengths without affecting others (see Figure 5.12).

Though the multiplexers and demultiplexers are mirror images of one another, there are key operating differences between the two. Multiplexers need to have nominal effect on the signals as they are being combined onto a fiber, so this calls for low insertion loss. They also need to insure that light isn't reflected or scattered back to any of the transmitters. Demultiplexers, on the other hand, need to be able to extract the optical channels from the multiplexed signal without light leaking from one channel to the next.

Just how many optical channels are packed onto a single fiber really depends. The ITU specified at least 100 GHz spacing between optical channels, which works out to be about 0.8-nm wavelengths for a total of 100 channels. So if there were three channels, for example, they could be located at the end of the 1500-nm band at 1530.33,

1531.12, and 1531.90, leaving small margin for computational rounding. Some proprietary systems pack the channels even closer at 50 GHz (0.4 nm), with developers looking at 25 (0.2 nm). It's not clear, however, when the latter will be available or even
whether the economics can really justify the additional connections. Certainly some
major carriers within the United States are looking at higher channel counts, but large
carriers outside of the United States are another matter (see "A View from the Field:
DWDM—Where Smaller and Cheaper Is Better").

A VIEW FROM THE FIELD:
DWDM—WHERE SMALLER AND CHEAPER IS BETTER

In the telecommunications industry, time has taught us that technology development is not necessarily aligned with reality. The hype that ac-
companied the Internet boom only made this more pronounced. For the
last five years, Internet growth drove considerable optical development
efforts, though perhaps not always in line with short-term expectations.

Key to these efforts was an interesting mix of strategic vision and a
bit of luck. Manufacturers enhanced DWDM systems to the point where
they could populate fiber with more than 300 10 Gbps wavelengths. At
the same time, substantial effort was spent in ultralong-haul capabilities,
enabling higher distances without electrical regeneration (> 2000 miles).

While these developments are feats of technical brilliance, where is
the market requirement? Who are the customers requesting them today?
Why? At what cost? What we really need are fewer channels at better
prices, not just more channels. We need longer distances—not ultra long,
but with better control and predictable performance characteristics.

The now infamous exponential IP traffic curve pushed many carriers
toward massive fiber builds and considerable DWDM backbone deployment. Expectations were that by the end of 2001 we'd be running backbones with 100 × 10 Gbps wavelengths—and barely keeping pace. It
never occurred!

Today, major routes in Europe are saturated with fiber. For example,
in some core links more than 500 fiber pairs are available, with less than
5 percent actually carrying traffic. Those fiber pairs that are operational
use terabit systems, but only at a fraction of their capacity. With that kind
of fiber inventory, carriers will be hard-pressed to recover their investment, and any value there may be further reduced through sales-driven
price erosion. At the same time, equipment vendors want us to use fiber

with more capacity at the cost of expensive hardware. They are promoting new wavelength capacity in the L-band (1565 to 1625 nm) in enhanced DWDM systems, which require expensive amplifiers and new sets of transponder wavelengths.

Enough already. Stop the madness. Today, the bandwidth race per fiber pair is over. We must concentrate on providing DWDM with additional management functionality (customer network management), resilience, flexibility, and provisioning capabilities.

Instead of putting more wavelengths per fiber, make systems cheaper and more manageable. Major capital cost has moved from fiber to DWDM equipment—from below 100 gigabits toward 1 terabit. The business case of 1997 and 1998, "optical DWDM vs. SDH space-division multiplexing," retrofitted with 2001 technology just isn't valid. Depending on fiber availability, distance, and cost we need to compromise between cheaper DWDM systems in multiple fibers and expensive enhanced DWDM in fewer fiber pairs. If fiber is available, ask a manufacturer which has a better return on investment: two C band (1530 to 1565nm) DWDM links in parallel, or one C+L band. A hybrid approach of standard and long-haul DWDM where required is probably the best answer. The technology choice must meet the business need.

Today, the business need is to meet the bottom line. This is unlikely to change. Huge, costly DWDM systems are a thing of the past. What we need is a new tagline for this industry: "Where Smaller & Cheaper Is Better"!

—By Pedro Falcao*

*Pedro Falcao Fonseca is currently the vice president of IP and optical network engineering at Ebone, a major pan-European carrier.

Of course, equipment developers aren't required to cram zillions of channels into a fiber. Those are just examples of one type of WDM, Dense-Wave-Division Multiplexing (DWDM). However, there are systems that have more than 200-GHz spacing; these are known **as Wide-Wavelength-Division Multiplexing** (**WWDM**). We saw the use of WWDM earlier with EFDAs, when a pump light was injected into an erbium fiber at a wavelength different from that of the incoming signal. Similarly, some system will use just two channels over a fiber in two different wavebands.

The difference in channel density has a big impact on the bottom line. As more channels are packed into fiber, components must work at higher tolerances. Fabry-Perot lasers, for example, get swapped out for DFB or DBR lasers with less **drift**. The result is that system costs increase significantly. This is a major reason why WDM systems being deployed in metro networks today utilize WWDM and not DWDM. We'll learn more about WDM metro in Chapter 8.

FILTERS ....

WDM systems work their magic through a combination of components, namely and gratings. Filters are devices that attenuate particular frequencies or wavelengths, but allow others to pass with relatively no change. Said differently, filters are components that can be incorporated along optical waveguides that are selectively transparent, allowing a range of frequencies through, but blocking others. This is particularly handy in dealing with DWDM systems where engineers want to isolate individual wavelengths.

While there are many different types of filters, six are regularly used in optical communications. These are interference or dielectric filters, dichroic filters, neutral-density filters, longpass and shortpass filters, and Bragg grating. We'll take each one individually.

- **Interference filters**—These are very useful in isolating frequencies for fiber optic telecommunication applications, because they operate in the wavelengths commonly used in optical networking, 1310 and 1550 nm. Two types of interference filters are important to WDM systems. **Band filters** reflect or transmit a range of wavelengths, around 20 or more. **Line filters** are fairly new phenomena and reflect or transmit a narrow range of wavelengths, such as one or two. There are two problems with interference filters. First, they are extremely angle sensitive, meaning that components require careful alignment for correct usage. Second, they significantly reduce throughput of the key wavelengths that they transmit.

- **Dichroic filters**—These are transparent substrates coated with thin films that selectively reflect or transmit various wavelengths. Dichroic filters are used in binoculars and camera lenses.

- **Neutral-density filters**—These are designed to reduce transmission evenly across a portion of the spectrum. Depending on the construction, they either absorb or reflect back the nontransmitted portion.

- **Longpass and shortpass filters**—These filters have a wavelength cutoff point. Longpass filters allow light having a wavelength greater than a certain value to pass, blocking shorter wavelengths. Shortpass filters allow light having a wavelength less than a certain value to pass, blocking longer wavelengths. If an amplifier is used with a pumping laser, a filter may be selected to allow the signal through, but to block the pumping wavelength. When several wavelengths are multiplexed down a fiber, a filter may be used to selectively transmit only certain wavelengths, blocking others.

FIBER BRAGG GRATINGS ....

Like filters, gratings also separate wavelengths from one another. They do this by using very fine lines scratched into the surface of a fiber or some other material. As the light pulse strikes the grating, the space between each adjacent pair of scratches either reflects or allows light to pass through, and constructive and destructive interference occurs, resulting in reflections or diffractions in particular directions only (see Figure 5.13). The exact direction depends on the slit separation and the wavelength of the incident light.

Fiber Bragg are probably the best-known gratings in optics. They're formed by exposing a piece of fiber made of ultraviolet (UV) sensitive glass to UV light via a diffraction grid that acts as a kind of stencil. In the region of the fiber where the UV light is incident, some of the bonds in the glass are broken. In this manner a regular variation in the microstructure of the piece of fiber is formed. Light having a wavelength similar to the periodic perturbation will be reflected back along the fiber, whereas light of other wavelengths will pass through unhindered.

So what's the difference between Fiber Bragg gratings and filters? To large extent it comes down to granularity and direction. Filters generally reflect back a larger range of frequencies than Fiber Bragg gratings while normally transmitting a narrower range of frequencies. Of course, the development of narrow-line filters muddles the waters a bit, but those general distinctions still hold true.

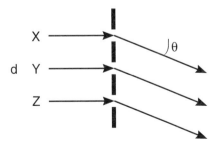

Figure 5.13
A diffraction grating.

There's another factor as well. By tilting a filter, the incident light is reflected away from the light source. With fiber gratings, however, the light is reflected back toward the light source.

Both sets of properties have very practical applications in system design. The properties of filters have made them well suited to WDM gear. As the channel density increases, manufacturers look at new ways of extracting more channels from a given fiber, hence the development of narrow-line filters.

Since Fiber Bragg gratings selectively reflect a narrow range of wavelengths, they are a natural choice for developing precision OADMs in a DWDM environment. Several gratings can then be built into a system to allow wavelengths to be combined or separated (see Figure 5.14).

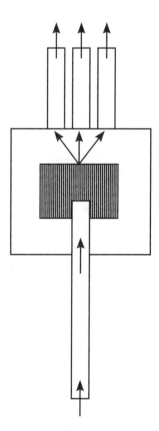

Figure 5.14
Transmission gratings can be used as beam splitters, enabling a single light signal to be split into three. Such an arrangement may be useful in networking, cable television, and the like.

Circulators

The problem, though, with using fiber gratings to isolate a wavelength is that the light gets reflected back toward the light source. The solution is to isolate a signal through a class of components known as **circulators**.

Circulators are somewhat akin to traffic circles. Like isolators used in EDFAs, they prevent light from flowing down a fiber, but instead of doing this for one fiber they work on three or four fibers.

Let's look, for example, at a three-port circulator. A signal coming in from port 1 is sent out via port 2, an incoming signal from port 2 is sent out through port 3, and one from port 3, as you've probably guessed, is sent out through port 1 (see Figure 5.15). To put that another way, the input fiber could be connected to port 1, a Fiber Bragg grating would be on port 2, and the output channel carrying the desired signal to be dropped on port 3.

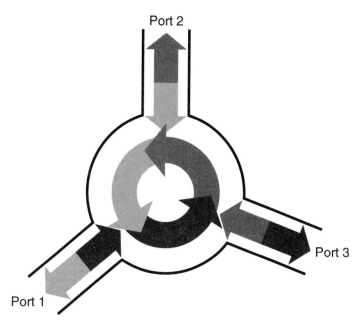

Figure 5.15
Circulators direct light from one fiber down another fiber.

OTHER COMPONENTS..

There are myriad of other components that you might hear about in the physical layer of the optical network. Some of the more significant ones are couplers and interferometers. Another, multiplexers, we'll cover at greater length in Chapter 6.

The word **coupler** has two meanings in fiber optics. Couplers are used for connecting waveguides (fibers) to light sources, detectors and the like. Couplers of this sort are sometimes called connectors.

Couplers are also devices that distribute optical power between ports. There are both passive and active couplers. Passive couplers, like fused fiber couplers, are used to join two fibers together, often when multiplexing signals. Active couplers, like repeaters, are used to produce two electrically separate output signals in networks.

Interferometers are instruments that employ the interference of light waves to measure the accuracy of optical surfaces, a property that comes in handy when testing and doing quality control of optical components during manufacturing. Light, as we know, is somewhat schizophrenic, behaving both as particles and as waves. Interferometry causes light from a coherent source to be split into two beams, which are made to interfere with each other. The resulting interference patterns indicate irregularities, such as surface roughness, on a scale comparable to that of the wavelength of light used.

SHORT CUTS..

Most of the components in the optical network are a type of semiconductors—those peculiar materials sitting somewhere between conductors (like metal), which conduct electricity, and insulators (like glass and plastic), which do not conduct electricity.

Two basic light sources are used—light-emitting diodes (LEDs) and lasers (Light Amplification by the Stimulated Emission of Radiation). The major difference comes down to reflective material used by lasers to build up a very powerful and precise beam of light.

Normally, electrons fall to a lower energy state, giving off the energy that we call light in a process called spontaneous emission. Lasers trap electrons in a high energy state in a process called stimulated emission.

Light detectors sit in the receivers of optical gear, enabling the equipment to translate the optical signal back to an electrical one.

Three types of devices address declining signal strength—amplifiers, regenerators, and repeaters. Amplifiers just increase the intensity of a signal detected, noise and all. Regenerators are more sophisticated, detecting the optical signal, converting it into an electronic signal, cleaning it up, and retransmitting it as an optical signal again, and are generally comprised of sophisticated electronics. Repeaters are also electro-optical devices, but, typically, they only provide amplification and reshaping, not full regeneration of a signal. Since the advent of all-optical ampfliers, repeaters are not commonly used in optical networks.

The two major types of amplifiers are Raman amplifiers and EDFAs. Raman amplifiers, based on the Raman effect, are more costly than EDFAs but provide optical gain throughout the low-loss fiber transmission window.

WDM systems combine multiple signals onto a single fiber and split them out of the fiber at the destination. There are two major categories. DWDM systems use less than 200 GHz spacing between channels for a total of 100 per channel, while WWDM systems use more than 200 GHz spacing between channels. WDM systems use a combination of components including filters and gratings.

6 Switching Technologies

In this chapter...

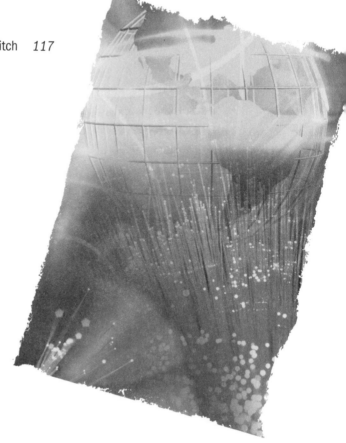

Without too much exaggeration, optical switches are probably the most important technologies today in developing the intelligent optical network. In conventional optical networks, wavelengths are configured for certain set routes. Carriers "nail up" circuits by configuring individual pieces of equipment, a process that takes weeks—even months—to occur. Yet with the growth of the Internet, customers need circuits provisioning in days or weeks, not months.

Enter optical switching. These boxes sit at fiber-to-fiber and fiber-to-copper junctures that can be remotely reconfigured on the fly to redirect signals coming from one port to any other port. This provisioning ideally occurs through software enabling carriers—in theory—to configure circuits in minutes.

Yet beyond that basic description, there are as many different switches as there are types of fibers that can connect to them. To simplify things, when we speak about optical switches in this chapter we'll mean only those switches operating at the Physical layer. Switches operating at higher layers, such as Ethernet switches, which we discussed in Chapter 2, will be revisited to some extent later in Chapter 10.

Even optical switches can be sliced and diced in different ways. Start out by understanding where switches sit in the network and their core functions. Some switches reside at the edge of the network, others in the network core. Then work through the basic switch architectures. Though optical switching is new, switches themselves have been around for years. The basic structural designs in a switch haven't changed much, and understanding the relative strengths and weaknesses of the approach is invaluable in pegging products in the field.

What has changed, though, are the materials and components used to build these switches. Optical switches employ some of the most exotic technologies around, from miniature mirrors to holograms to bubbles. We'll take a look at them and their respective strengths and weaknesses.

SWITCHING JOBS

Optical switches play several key roles in the network. Broadly speaking, we can group these functions into restoration, transport, and testing.

- **Restoration**—Automatic protection switching techniques direct network traffic around component failures or fiber cuts by situating switches at critical junctures in the network.

- **Transport**—Switches play two key roles in directing traffic within the network. Optical add-drop multiplexers (OADMs) use switching elements to extract specific wavelengths as determined by a network designer. Meshed network use switches to interconnect incoming lines. More specifically, edge switches interconnect and combine incoming low-speed lines for delivery onto an OC-3 or OC-12 trunk. **Optical or photonic crossconnects**, also called **photonic switches**, or **wavelength routing**, sit at critical junctures within the core of the network moving the capacity of fibers, wavebands, or individual wavelengths between ports.

- **Testing and network management**—Switches are also used in testing individual components, where each switched lightpath reflects a given testing parameter. Similarly, testing devices, like Optical Time-Domain Reflectometers (OTDRs), use switching elements to monitor multiple fibers at remote sites or to monitor active traffic unobtrusively.

THE SMART SWITCH

AFTER TWO DECADES OF LABOR, VICTOR AND MELVIN'S STAR SWITCH MAKES FOR THE BIG TIME.

OOO AND OEO SWITCHES ....

When designing an optical network, the area that's garnered a lot of interest is the use of switching with transport. These switches are classified broadly as **all-optical switches**, also called transparent, photonic, or **OOO** (optical-optical-optical) switches, and optical-electrical switches, also called opaque or **OEO** (optical-electrical-optical) switches. All optical switches receive an optical signal on one side, switch it, and send light out the other side. Optical-electrical switches receive optical signals on one side, convert them into electrical form, and do some processing—perhaps looking up addresses in a routing database if the switching includes router functionality or some other functions—and then retransmit those optical signals on the other side. OOO switches tend to move the capacities of whole fibers between ports. OEO switches usually can differentiate between individual wavelengths. Switch manufacturers are looking at ultimately switching the very photons that comprise packets without translating them into electrical form, though that's still more science fiction than fact.

At some point in the far distant future, optical networks might very well be purely photonic between end points, but today there are some very good reasons for having electrons and photons in the network. All-optical switches are bit-rate and protocol transparent, so with a single interface the switch can support any kind of traffic. They switch huge capacities blazingly fast. They also avoid the high costs associated with converting between electrical and optical domains. These factors make them well suited to the core of the network as all-optical crossconnects.

Optical-electrical switches today address a different set of problems. Since they convert the signal into electrical form, they can extract network management information and regenerate the signal. Neither of those functions can be done today in the optical domain.

Optical-electrical architectures are also particularly good in forming grooming switches. A **grooming switch** looks inside an incoming STM-n stream, identifies the destination of the multiplexed channels, and then reorganizes the channels so they can be delivered to their destinations more efficiently (see Figure 6.1). By contrast, multiplexing combines the frames together onto an output port without regard for the destination.

At one time it was thought that transparent switches would be needed to reach high-port densities. Top densities on opaque switches were limited to around 256 ports. Advancements in silicon, however, reduced those differences; today, opaque switches reach up to densities of 1,024 ports. Transparent switches still tout higher port densities, up to 4,000 ports or so, but often require the use of immature technologies entailing higher risk than conventional, silicon techniques used in opaque switching. The additional scalability of opaque switches may not obviate the need for transparent switching, but it has enabled carriers to postpone transparent switch deployments.

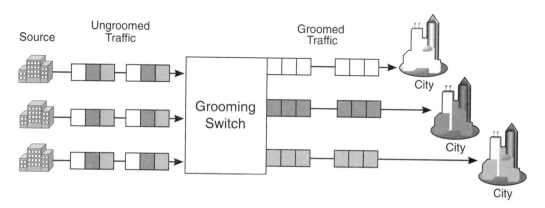

Figure 6.1
With grooming switches, traffic is reorganized for maximum delivery efficiency.

Yet, as opaque switching can't provide all of scalability and the protocol independence of transparent switching, the two technologies are likely to persist. Opaque switches being used at the access to groom traffic, transparent switches used in the network core to either aggregate to higher port speeds, like OC-48 to OC-192, or to provide traffic rerouting, without converting to the electrical domain (see Figure 6.2).

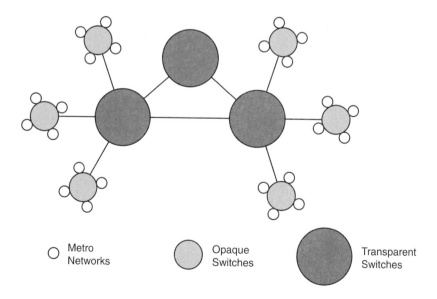

Figure 6.2
Transparent switches reside in the core of the network surrounded by opaque switches, which consolidate traffic from incoming metro core networks.

Of course those are simplistic representations. The increasing capacities of opaque switches enable carriers to extend them further and further into the core network. At the same time, as vendors add DWDM and routing intelligence to edge switches, more wavelengths become available to those switches with better grooming possibilities. This may increase the opportunity for photonic switching in the network.

BUILDING THE OPTICAL SWITCH ....

Though optical switching is fairly new, the idea of switching is very old, and the basic architecture for designing a switch remains largely the same. The simplest switch is the optical crossconnect (OXC) that takes wavelengths on one input port and switches them to one or more output ports.

There are two types of crossconnects, or space-division switches as they're technically known: permutation and generalized. **Permutation switches** consist of point-to-point links between different ports. One-to-many connections aren't possible—the number of connections that are possible are a factor of adding up the total number of two-pair combinations—they are permutations, hence the category's name (see Figure 6.3).

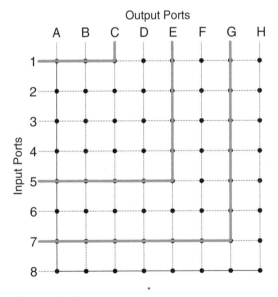

Figure 6.3
With permutation switches, only point-to-point links are allowed.

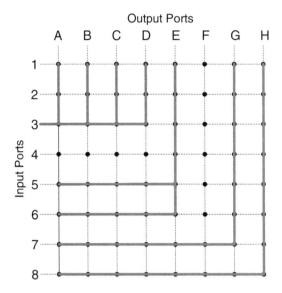

Figure 6.4
With generalized switches, point-to-point (8–H), point-to-multipoint (3–A, B, and C), and multipoint-to-point (5 and 6–E) connections are all possible.

    Generalized switches, however, can connect one input port to many output ports or many input ports to one output. The result is significantly more switch combinations (see Figure 6.4) Special generalized switches, called **linear divider-combiners (LDCs)** go a step further and enable carriers to divide up the input power among the output ports for better attenuation characteristics.

Dr. Geek on...
Switching

Ever wonder just how many connections a switch permutation or generalized switch can make? There are some pretty easy ways to figure. With an $n \times n$ switch, permutation switches will only support the factorial of n connections. This is because only point-to-point links are supported. So with our 8×8 port switch we'd have $8 \times 7 \times 6 \times 5 \times 4 \times 3 \times 2 \times 1$ or 40,320 possible connections.

    Thinks that's a lot? Just consider generalized switches. Since point-to-multipoint connections and multipoint-to-point connections are allowed, generalized switches have far more possible connections. Where a switch has n input port and y output ports, the number of connection states with generalized switches is calculated by 2^{ny} or, in more other-worldly terms, 18,446,744,073,709,600,000 connections.

Additionally, generalized switches and LDCs can terminate a signal internally, while permutation switches cannot. This means that networks of permutation switches get to be very tricky. Switches can inadvertently create connections that cause all sorts of headaches. With a WDM network, for example, closed paths can form rings for certain wavelengths. Lots of WDM networks are amplified, and amplifiers generate small amounts of noise. With a ring, the noise accumulates and grows very large, interfering with or taking power from other wavelengths.

BASIC DESIGN TYPES ....

There are a couple of ways of building these switches. The simplest approach is the **crossbar switch** shown in Figures 6.2 and 6.3. The input and output ports cross over one another, forming a kind of net. With electronic switches, the crossbar could be traced on a printed circuit board using electronic gates. Optical switches have adopted the same basic design, using optical couplers instead of gates. By controlling the position of these couplers, connections can be made between two different ports.

The biggest problem with the crossbar is in the number of crosspoints. With a switch having 100 input ports and 100 output ports, not unheard of in the core of the network, the resulting number of crosspoints would be 100^2 or 10,000 points. Each point requires optical splitters or combiners, increasing the cost of the system.

All of these are good reasons to interject small crossbars as elements in designing a large crossbar switch. With this design, called a **Clos architecture**, three tiers of connections occur. The input ports connect to one set of crossbars, the output ports to another, and both sets of crossbars are connected to a third set (see Figure 6.5).

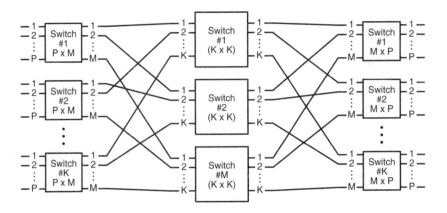

Figure 6.5
Clos architecture of an *N x N* switch.

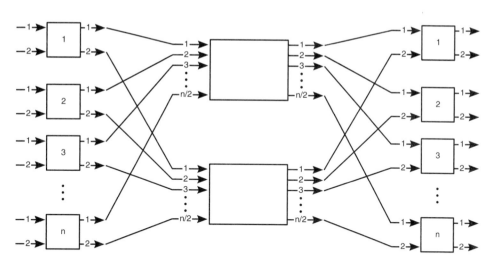

Figure 6.6
Recursion for Benes switch.

With permutation switches, the Clos structure can be devolved further into a **Benes switch fabric** where a series of 2×2 switches are used for any combination. Basically, the idea is that any one of the middle switches can be described as having half the number of input and output ports on either end (see Figure 6.6).

These in turn can be divided into two switches until you reach a whole mess of 2×2 couplers (see Figure 6.7). Although the Benes architecture is close to optimal use of hardware, switch developers prefer to use larger switching elements and not 2×2 couplers, which at some point raise scalability problems.

Generalized and LDC switches play off similar architectures. Generalized switches use a crossbar design but involve more switching elements within the switch. This is because the generalized switch can support more than just a point-to-point connection. Crossbars, however, introduce signal attenuation from the two stages of splitting and combining signals. LDCs correct the problem by introducing controllable power-dividing and power-combining stages.

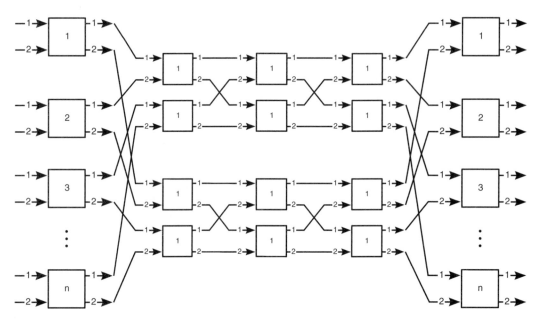

Figure 6.7
An 8 x 8 Benes switch.

TO BLOCK OR NOT TO BLOCK..............................

Switch manufacturers often talk about the **blocking** characteristics of their switches. The idea here can be readily understood if we think of an old mechanical switch with two arms that connect ports on either side of the device. Any port can speak with any other port, but, depending on the speed of the switching element, some connections might be unable to be connected, or blocked (see Figure 6.8).

There are three nonblocking categories, which differ in their hardware simplicity, control complexity, and connection impact. **Rearrangeably nonblocking switches** might have to move existing connections in the switching matrix around to accommodate a new connection. N N switches are rearrangeably nonblocking. This means adding the necessary logic to figure out the path across the switching matrix is not always a simple thing. Existing connections might need to be interrupted to enable rerouting to occur. As a result, they are relatively simple in their hardware design, but introduce a high degree of control complexity and have a relatively high impact on connections.

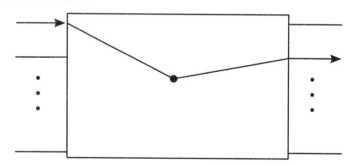

Figure 6.8
Blocking refers to the ability of the switch to connect all ports simultaneously.
With this old crossbar switch, for example, only two ports can be connected
at once; the rest are blocked.

Wide-sense nonblocking switches, like the Clos-type architecture, avoid rearranging active connections altogether, but only if the right rules for routing new connections are used. More hardware is needed to implement this additional complexity and routing algorithms are needed, but there's no effect on existing connections.

Strict-sense nonblocking switches, like Clos and Benes architectures, skip the rerouting hardware complexity and the connection routing. New connections can use any free path in the switch. The tradeoff here, though, is that even more hardware than wide-sense nonblocking switches must be used (see Table 6.1).

Table 6.1   Merits of Nonblocking Approach

Type	Hardware Cost	Connection Algorithm Complexity	Existing Connection Impact
Rearrangeable	Low	High	High
Wide-Sense	Medium	High	Low
Strict-Sense	High	Low	Low

Each of these approaches has a role to play. Where lots of connections need to be established and torn down in the network, like the metro core, rearrangeable and wide-sense architectures require an overwhelming amount of computational complexity. As fewer connections are used, as in the long-haul, rearrangeable and wide-sense architectures may become more popular.

MEASURING UP ....

While blocking is certainly one aspect of evaluating switch technology, there are other items to consider as well. These include the size of the switching matrix, scalability, switching granularity, switching speed, and loss.

- **Matrix size**—As there are potentially a huge number of lines coming into a location, the sheer number of ports that the switch can support is critical. Today switches can reach 4000 × 4000 ports that's four thousand input ports and four thousand output ports, but no doubt for some applications that's overkill. Others have taken to targeting small sizes, such as 64 × 64 ports.

- **Scalability**—Many providers utilize architectures or switching that top out at several dozen ports. Remember the Clos and Benes designs. If a provider delivers a small switch based around 2 × 2 switching elements, for example, scaling to larger port counts will quickly require very complex switching elements in the core of the switch.

- **Granularity**—The size of those ports needs to be closely examined. Are carriers supporting OC-3, OC-12, OC-48, or OC-192 ports? What are their plans for OC-768? Even the whole discussion of ports in some cases can be misleading. With optical crossconnects, port counts make sense because they only connect individual fibers together. Not so with a wavelength router, where the number of wavelengths that are switched is key.

  Speaking about wavelengths, determining whether a switch works on wavelength or fiber levels is important. Also important, though, is whether switches can grow gracefully up to large port counts. Huge jumps in port counts force higher expenditures than might be necessary.

- **Switching Speed**—Just how fast must switches be to move light from one port to another? The short answer is, it depends. Currently, switching within milliseconds is sufficient. SONET fails over to backup links within 50 milliseconds, unbeknownst to higher-layer protocols. Ultimately, though, switches are targeting moving individual packets photonically, in which case nanosecond switching times are required.

- **Loss**—Loss is the enemy of any network designer. When it comes to switching, loss can result from coupling the fiber and switch together as well as the matrix itself. Optical switch losses can range from around 1 or 2 dB to 4 or 5 dB.

TECHNOLOGIES FOR BUILDING THE OPTICAL SWITCH ·······································

All sorts of fascinating and exciting technologies are used today for building optical switching elements. The basic idea, though, remains the same: how to redirect a light signal in different directions through the application of energy in some form. These technologies are: microelectromechanical systems (MEMs), optomechanical switches, thermo-optic switches, bubble-based switches, liquid crystals, acousto-optics and electrically switchable Bragg gratings. We'll look at each of these separately.

MEMS

Imagine a huge hall of mirrors the size of a warehouse, filled with hundreds, even thousands of mirrors. Someone steps into the hall on one end, and instantly the image projects onto mirrors on the other end.

That's pretty much the way a MEMS switch operates, but on a much smaller scale. With MEMS technology, a single substrate hosts hundreds of miniature mirrors that are tilted back and forth within microseconds. Optical signals striking these miniature mirrors are reflected to the appropriate output port.

MEMS-based switches come in two, three, and four dimensions. Mirrors in two-dimensional MEMS switches flip up or down (see Figure 6.9). Mirrors in three-di-

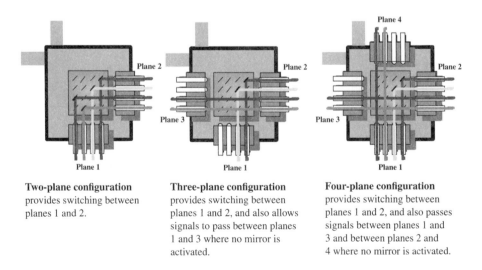

Two-plane configuration provides switching between planes 1 and 2.

Three-plane configuration provides switching between planes 1 and 2, and also allows signals to pass between planes 1 and 3 where no mirror is activated.

Four-plane configuration provides switching between planes 1 and 2, and also passes signals between planes 1 and 3 and between planes 2 and 4 where no mirror is activated.

Figure 6.9
Sample MEMS configuration (Courtesy of OMM Inc., San Diego, CA).

mensional switches can redirect light in three directions, and those in four dimensions can switch between ports on four planes.

With MEMS switches there are a few challenges to be aware of. Perhaps the biggest is long-term reliability. It's unclear as to how long these individual mirrors will last before the parts wear out and lose their precise positioning.

Signal loss is also a big concern. MEMS designs typically lose several decibels when light passes through the switch. To put that in perspective, a five decibel loss would mean that just 32 percent of input power remains. Some newer MEMS designs are claiming significantly lower loss-characteristics, on the order of a decibel or less.

Finally, large port density remains elusive. Though there are MEMS switches that have over 16×16 ports, doing so typically sacrifices on reliability. The big challenge remains in how to change the angle of reflection, a technology that is still maturing.

Optomechanical Switches

An approach similar to MEMS is to use a movable piece of fiber to redirect signals from one port to another. This approach, called **optomechanical switches**, use a mechanical slider that moves fiber or some other component to focus the signal on a particular output port. By latching the component into position, light can pass from input ports to output ports (see Figure 6.10).

The idea is simple enough, but creating optomechanical switches is highly demanding. Switching components must be moved precisely. Even slightly misdirecting a signal can prevent proper functioning.

Still, optomechanical approaches are widely used, because they are the simplest to implement. Often they have a role where optical switching isn't frequently done, as when switching around a failed component. Some test equipment uses this kind of optical switching technology as well.

Figure 6.10
Optomechanical switching.

Electro-Optical and Thermo-Optic Switches

By utilizing the electro-optic effect, components vendors have created responsive, but small, switches. The electro-optic effect basically says that there will be a change in the refractive index (RI) of certain materials when an electric field is applied. This change affects the velocity of the passing light almost immediately. Since light's velocity in a material is the speed of light divided by the RI, increasing the RI slows light's velocity, and reducing RI increases the signal's speed.

Electro-optic switches consist of two couplers with an active section in the middle of one or both links (see Figure 6.11). By applying an electric field to one section, light can be shifted in phase by 180° and moved to another port. By applying a comparable field to both signals, the signals can be swapped between ports.

The big win with the electro-optic effect is the speed at which switching occurs. The problem, however, is one of scale. Electro-optical technology is effective for 2×2 switches, but building larger switches is more difficult.

Thermo-optical switches use a similar principle, but instead of applying an electrical field to change the characteristics of the fiber, the temperature is changed with a similar effect. Two types of thermo-optical switches are on the market today. Interferometric switches are smaller, but their performance depends on the wavelengths traveling through them. As a result, they often need some sort of control to precisely maintain the temperature on the individual link. Digital optical switches (DOSs), however, are more robust. The simplest are 1×2 switches. By increasing the temperature in one arm, the RI increases and blocks the light from passing through. Accordingly, a less precise temperature needs to be reached and maintained.

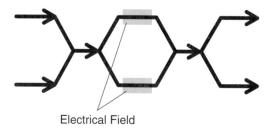

Electrical Field

Figure 6.11
An electro-optical switch.

Bubble Switches

Have you even imagined that the inkjet printer might one day sit in the core of the public network, responsible for connecting millions of conversations across the planet? Probably not, especially since inkjet printers seem to have a problem with several dozen pages a minute, let alone a few million connections a second. Yet the underlying technology of an inkjet printer can be used to form highly scalable and effective optical switches.

The idea is to use two sets of silicon strips. A bottom layer consists of microscopic trenches etched into the silicon, intersecting one another. These trenches are waveguides for directing the incoming light and are filled with special fluid having the same refractive index as the silica. A top layer contains electrodes for heating the liquid and forming a gas bubble (see Figure 6.12).

Normally light travels right through this liquid as it would through glass, but when a bubble is formed at one of the intersections, light is redirected down one of the channels. Each gas bubble has an RI that's much lower than that of the liquid and beyond the critical angle at which total internal reflection occurs.

The good news here is that bubble switches don't have any moving parts, so there aren't the same concerns with reliability that face MEMs or optomechanical switches. The real problem is that today bubble technology remains in its infancy.

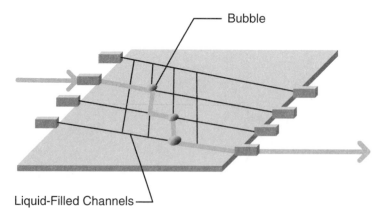

Figure 6.12
By stimulating liquid-filled channels at critical junctures with electrical nodes (not shown), light is deflected to another channel and ultimately to an output port.

Liquid Crystals

If bubble switches can steal a thing or two from printer technology, then liquid-crystal-based switches can steal from monitor or wristwatch technology. The same basic substance used in building laptop monitors or digital watch displays can be used for redirecting light to different ports, albeit with a bit more technology thrown in.

The key here is the nature of liquid crystals. Typically, molecules within materials align themselves randomly. Liquid crystals, however, are different. They have well-defined molecular alignments, with the cigar-shaped molecules forming the substance pointing in the same direction, called the optic axis. By applying a voltage to the liquid crystal, these molecules can be made to shift position, changing certain properties, such as their refractive index (RI). The ability to change molecular alignment and RI means liquid crystals can be used in some interesting ways when it comes to switching. Exactly how depends on the particular design of the switch.

At one time, liquid crystal design was polarization dependent. **Polarization** in light waves, as we saw earlier, is the direction in which the electric field vibrates. Linearly polarized light consists of light waves where electric fields vibrate in the same direction all the time. Elliptically or circularly polarized light occurs when the plane within which the electrical field vibrates rotates around the wave's axis.

These liquid crystal switches use a multistage process to move light between input and output ports. Initially, an incoming light wave strikes a lens that divides the polarized signal into two rays of opposite polarity. Both rays strike liquid crystal components and are reflected back toward another lens, where the two beams are recombined. Each of the liquid crystal elements has electrodes attached. Depending on the voltage applied by the electrodes, the polarity of the signals can be changed, ultimately altering the outbound port (see Figure 6.13).

Polarization-Dependent Liquid Crystal Switch

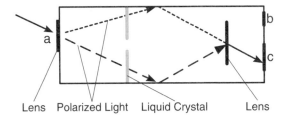

Lens   Polarized Light   Liquid Crystal   Lens

Figure 6.13

When light enters port a it goes through a lens that splits the light into its polarized components. They travel through a liquid crystal device that contains electrical charges. Depending on the field provided, the polarity of the light signals changes, and when they are recombined at the output, they get directed to b or c.

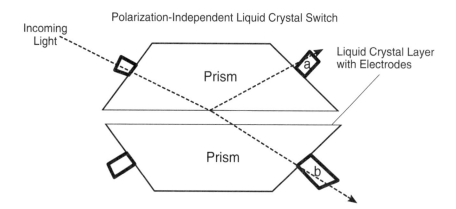

Figure 6.14
Depending on the voltage applied to the liquid crystal layer, the incoming light is either reflected through port a or it passes through to port b.

A new wrinkle uses liquid crystals for their reflective properties. With this design, a liquid crystal layer and electrodes sit between two prisms. Two input and two output ports are attached to the opposite sides of the prism. When a light ray enters from an input port, it strikes the boundary between the prisms and the liquid crystal layer. Depending on the voltage applied to the layer, the liquid crystal either reflects the light back into the prism and toward one output port or allows the light to pass through to the next prism to the other output port (see Figure 6.14).

Liquid crystal technology offers several benefits. Reliability is expected to be very good, as there are no moving parts. What's more, larger port count switches are possible, though today only 2×2 switches are available. Loss can be a problem, and one reason stated for reflective design is that it offers less loss than the former approach. Power consumption is very low, but at times heating crystals to increase switching performance can increase power requirements.

Disappearing Act

Two technologies out there are developing ways to make Bragg gratings appear and disappear by applying an electrical voltage. **Electroholographic switches** imbed holographic images of Bragg gratings within special crystals, called KLTNs (potassium lithium tantalata niobate). These crystals are arranged in rows and columns: The rows represent individual fibers; the columns represent the wavelengths. Each crystal is electrically controlled. Normally light just passes right through the crystals without a problem, but when a voltage is applied and the hologram is activated, the incoming light is diverted to a specific output port.

Electroholography might have a bright future (no pun intended). There are no moving parts, so reliability should be pretty good. The technology is very scalable and switching speeds are really fast. Losses are also very low. Power consumption can be a bit on the high side, however.

The second technology, called **electrically switchable Bragg gratings** (ESBGs, pronounced "ess-bugs"), works on a similar principle. Here, though, to make the grating "appear," droplets of liquid crystal are applied to a polymer and placed over a waveguide. When there's no voltage, the grating deflects a defined wavelength traveling in the waveguides. When voltage is applied, the grating disappears, and light travels through normally.

ESBGs put up some pretty respectable numbers if proponents are to be believed. Switching speeds are on the order of about 100 microseconds, which makes them significantly faster than MEMs or bubble switches. Losses are supposed to be around 1 dB and power consumption around 50 milliwatts.

Acousto-Optics

Sound can also be used as the basis of an optical switch, with some pretty impressive results. **Acousto-optic switches** capitalize on technology used today in movie screen projectors. The idea is to use acoustic waves to create regions in a solid of higher and lower densities. These densities can deflect passing light beams at different angles. By altering the acoustic patterns, optical signals are moved between ports.

The technology delivers blazingly fast switching speeds, between 500 nanoseconds and 10 microseconds, and potentially very good reliability, since there are no moving parts. Nor, for that matter, are there many vendors implementing the technology.

WAVELENGTH CONVERSION ....

Until now we've been concerned primarily with switches where the input and output signals are on the same wavelength, but in the future look for wavelength converters to be deployed.

Today, optical switching occurs on a common wavelength. If a transmission bound for New York leaves San Francisco on 1565 nm, then the transmission arrives in New York at 1565 nm.

However, there's an obvious need to be able to move transmission between wavelengths. The need arises because carriers may not have a wavelength available end to end. They would then like to carry a transmission, say, on 1586.2 from San Francisco to Chicago, and then on wavelength 1565 from Chicago to New York (see Figure 6.15).

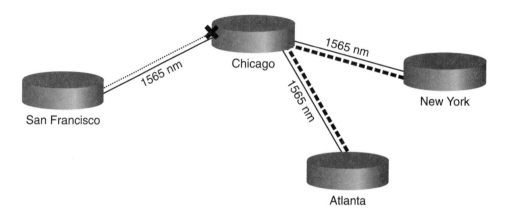

Figure 6.15
With current technology, the same wavelength must be used for end-to-end communications. In this instance, since Atlanta is communicating with New York via the 1565nm wavelength, San Francisco's transmission is blocked.

Working that lane-jumping magic today requires first converting the wavelength into the electrical domain. Opto-electro conversions are inherently expensive. All-optical wavelength converters might ultimately be cheaper, but such products are still largely at the stage of lab research.

SHORT CUTS...

Switches fill a number of different roles. As OADMs (optical add-drop multiplexers), they enable individual wavelengths to be extracted from a DWDM link. As grooming switches, they aggregate low-speed traffic onto an OC-3 or OC-12 line. Within the core, they are the optical crossconnects, interconnecting lots of incoming lines.

Switches can work on granularities of individual fibers, wavebands, or wavelengths.

Switches can be categorized as transparent and opaque. Transparent switches never convert the signal back to the electrical domain, saving the cost of those expensive conversions. Opaque switches convert back to the electrical domain, providing for better network management and signal regeneration.

The key criteria in evaluating the physical functionality of a switch are the size of the switching matrix, scalability, switching granularity, switching speed, and loss.

Major techniques in building optical switches are: microelectromechanical systems (MEMs), optomechanical switches, thermo-optic switches, bubble-based switches, liquid crystals, acousto-optics, and electrically switchable Bragg gratings.

Part III

7 The SONET Factor

In this chapter…

Think public network technology and think SONET. For nearly 20 years, the Synchronous Optical NETwork has been the transport of choice for today's public network. It's easy to see why. Highly resilient and well adapted for predictable, time-sensitive traffic, SONET complemented the voice traffic carried by the phone providers.

Data's increasing presence, however, is changing carrier requirements. The changes in traffic patterns are leading to new technologies for building metro networks. At the same SONET is adapting to the challenge.

Only by understanding the traditional positioning of SONET, however, can we understand the significance of these new technologies. This means a close look at the state of the public network before SONET's arrival, the SONET hierarchy, and the operation of the protocol.

Throughout our discussion, though, a bit of cold realism is needed. Telecom's 20-year love affair with SONET is hardly a one-night stand. SONET remains the only viable solution for deploying large-scale, highly resilient, revenue-producing networks. Limitations and all, the protocol is the choice for traditional telecom operators. Will that change? No doubt it will—and we'll look at the competing technological solutions over the remaining chapters. Today, though, old and crusty SONET has one feather in its telecom hat and perhaps the only one that matters. It works.

LIFE BEFORE SONET..

Back in Chapter 1 we lied, but just a little bit. We said that SONET formed our first-generation optical network, but in fact there were optics before SONET. Call it the prehistoric age of telecommunications, where proprietary architectures and multiplexing formats ruled. Back then the users of this equipment—the Regional Bell Operating Companies (RBOCS) and interexchange carriers (IXCs) in the United States, Canada, Korea, Taiwan, and Hong Kong—wanted standards so they could mix and match equipment from different suppliers. SONET was the answer in the United States and ultimately was globally standardized as Synchronous Data Hierarchy (SDH) by the International Telecommunications Union—Telecommunication Sector (ITU-T), a United Nations technical subcommittee. SONET and SDH are nearly identical, though there are significant enough differences that equipment vendors must explicitly indicate whether they support SONET, SDH, or both on a port card. We'll focus on the SONET standard here.

Though the protocol didn't completely eliminate the proprietary gear pervading the public network, SONET did radically improve the situation, creating defined physical, management, and operational interfaces. More specifically SONET enabled:

- a reduction in equipment requirements and an increase in network reliability
- precise performance monitoring and fault detection, facilitating centralized fault isolation
- synchronous multiplexing format that greatly simplified interfacing to other equipment
- automatic protection switching to protect against outages caused by cable cuts and equipment failures
- the creation of a set of generic standards to interconnect different vendors' equipment
- the definition of a flexible architecture capable of accommodating future applications, with a variety of transmission rates. These rates are called optical carrier (OC) levels and electrically equivalent synchronous transport signals (STSs) for the fiber optic based transmission hierarchy

A Matter of Time

Prior to SONET, transmission systems within the United States were asynchronous, with each piece of equipment running its own clock. Clocking is so important in digital systems because equipment needs to keep the bit rate constant in order to know where ones and zeros begin. As you can imagine, an everyday Timex won't work as the clock for these synchronous networks. A highly reliable clock is needed to precisely sample the network. This is particularly true at very high data rates, where the interval to sample a network and read a bit falls down to the microseconds. Synchronous network use a Stratum 1 Primary Reference Clock (PRC), accurate to better than +/– 1 part in 10^{-11} and derived from a cesium atomic standard.

Even if two Stratum clocks are remarkably well synchronized, what we call plesiochronous or almost synchronous, large variations can occur in the clock rate. A DS-3 (44.736 Mbits/s) at 20 ppm (parts per million) can produce a variation of 1789 Bits/s between one incoming DS-3 and another.

With synchronous signals, like SONET, the digital transitions between bits in the signals occur at exactly the same rate, though, within set tolerance, they may occur at slightly different times. These differences, called phase differences, may be due to the time it takes a signal to travel down a wire or changes in timing between signals, a problem called jitter, due to the transmission network. By contrast, transitions with the plesiochronous signals occur at "almost" the same rate, with any variation being constrained within tight limits. Asynchronous signals do not necessarily transit at the same nominal rate.

As we mentioned back in Chapter 1, SONET—and for that matter asynchronous equipment—work on a network of multiplexers and demultiplexers. Transmissions from different lines are combined together in a box, a multiplexer, and sent on their way on a higher-speed line. At the other end the line gets demultiplexed, and the signals are broken out and delivered to their appropriate destination.

When asynchronous equipment sends information, it does so in stages. Twenty four DS-0s (64 Kbits/s) lines are multiplexed up to a DS-1 (1.544 Mbits/s). Four DS-1s are in turn muxed onto a DS-2 (6.312 Mbits/s), seven DS-2s onto a DS-3 (44.736 Mbits/s), and so forth. If you're doing the math, something will look a bit funny about those numbers. They don't really add up. Twenty four DS-0s should be 1.536 Mbits/s, not 1.544 Mbits/s. Seven DS-2s should be 44.184 Mbits/s, not 44.736 Mbits/s.

The problem is the synchronization. Remember, these systems are at best *plesio-*chronous. They're almost synchronized, but not quite. As such, the transmissions can't be combined precisely. Some additional bits need to be added during multiplexing, a process called bit stuffing, for the signals to be accurately read. At higher speeds these rates require more bits to be stuffed and more capacity to be lost.

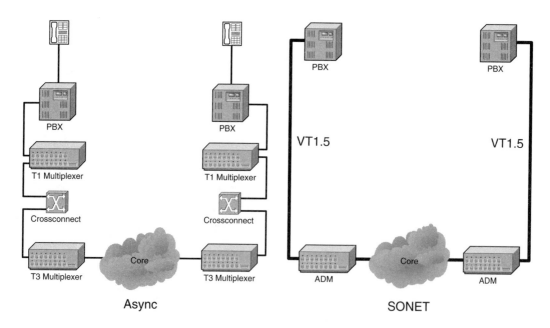

Figure 7.1
With async communications, a string of equipment is needed to demultiplex a signal. SONET enables the same functionality with far less equipment.

The other problem is demuxing. As these signals reach higher rates, the individual channels cannot be accessed without demultiplexing the entire sequence. This forces the provider to purchase and maintain a large amount of multiplexing equipment on either end for muxing and demuxing signals at each stage moving from DS-0 to DS-1, DS-2, and then to a DS-3. Each end also requires crossconnects to interconnect the different channels from the multiplexers, making a kind of tree (see Figure 7.1).

The SONET Hierarchy

SONET changed all of that. The use of a single clock enabled SONET gear to neatly combine channels together. To describe how these channels can be combined, SONET defines a hierarchy of three classes of capacities that can be used for transmitting and receiving SONET information. The smallest channel increments are the **virtual tributaries (VTs)**, which add up into **synchronous transport signals (STSs)** for electrical interface and **optical carrier (OC)** for optical interfaces.

The unit on which these clocks work is the STS-1/OC-1 (51.84 Mbits/s). Two STS-1s/OC-1s can be combined, forming an STS-2/OC-2, and when three are combined, an STS-3/OC-3 is formed. This grouping forms the STS family and is known as the lower-order SONET links.

Under SDH things are a little different. STS-1s can also be combined to form larger capacities called STMs. The smallest STM is equal to an STS-3 (155.520 Mbits/s). The largest STM signal today is specified at STM-256 (39.81 Gbits/s) (see Table 7.1).

Table 7.1   SONET Hierarchy

Optical Level	Electrical Level	Level of Concatenation	Line Rate (Mbps)	Maximum Payload Rate (Mbps)	Maximum Overhead Rate (Mbps)	SDH Equivalent
OC-1	STS-1	-	51.840	50.112	1.728	-
OC-3	STS-3	3 x STS-1	155.520	150.336	5.184	STM-1
OC-9	STS-9	3 x STS-3	466.560	451.008	15.552	STM-3
OC-12	STS-12	4 x STS-3	622.080	601.344	20.736	STM-4
OC-18	STS-18	6 x STS-3	933.120	902.016	31.104	STM-6
OC-24	STS-24	8 x STS-3	1244.160	1202.688	41.472	STM-8
OC-36	STS-36	12 x STS-3	1866.240	1804.032	62.208	STM-13

Table 7.1   SONET Hierarchy (Continued)

Optical Level	Electrical Level	Level of Concatenation	Line Rate (Mbps)	Maximum Payload Rate (Mbps)	Maximum Overhead Rate (Mbps)	SDH Equivalent
OC-48	STS-48	26 x STS-3	2488.320	2405.376	82.944	STM-16
OC-96	STS-96	32 x STS-3	4976.640	4810.752	165.888	STM-32
OC-192	STS-192	64 x STS-3	9953.280	9621.504	331.776	STM-64
OC-768*	STS-768	256 x STS-3	39813.12	38486.016	1327.104	STM-256

In process

To reach smaller granularities of bandwidth, STS-1s are broken down into VTs. There are four types of VTs: VT-1 .5, VT-2, VT-3, and VT-6. Actually the name VT is appropriate, as these are the small feeder links "flowing" from corporate offices to the larger lines like streams flowing into a larger river (see Table 7.2).

Table 7.2   The VT Hierarchy

VT Type	Bit Rate	Number of VTs in a VT Group	Number of VTs in an STS-1
VT1.5	1.728 Mbits/s	4	28
VT2	2.403 Mbits/s	3	21
VT3	3.456 Mbits/s	2	14
VT6	6.912 Mbits/s	1	7

SONET Configurations

These channels are mapped onto the three basic network types—point-to-point, hub, and ring—that we saw back in Chapter 2. Each has its unique benefits. Point-to-point links are the least expensive to implement. Hub networks provide tremendous flexibility. Ring networks offer very high resiliency. To get a better feel for where these might be used in the network, let's look at a connection running between a company's headquarters and a branch office (see Figure 7.2).

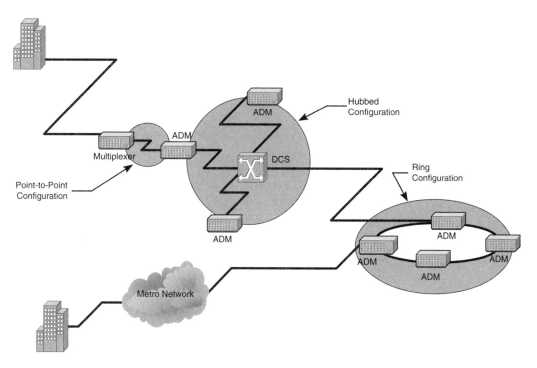

Figure 7.2
Three SONET configurations.

When a company connects two offices, each say with a T1, what happens? Very simplistically, the provider provides a T1 line to each office. The time slots are assigned at the various junctures, providing a circuit between the two premises

Assuming SONET is terminated at the perimeter of the carrier's network, the provider could use a simple point-to-point configuration to connect the two offices. With this design, a multiplexer, called a path termination element, sits at the edge of the network, takes the T-1 signals coming from the customer, and multiplexes them together to form an STS-1.

This new signal then travels through an **add-drop multiplexer (ADM)** digital crossconnect system (DCS, pronounced D-A-X). ADMs enable providers to demultiplex the specific channel that's required for a connection to the network. The DCS switches slots between ports on the same or different ADMs based on certain rules and parameters configured by the operators. Narrowband DCS switch channels up to DS0 (64 Kbits/s); Wideband DCS switch up to DS1 (1.544 Mbits/s) and Broadband DCS switch DS3s (44.736 Mbits/s).

SONET Protection

Once the information leaves the DCS, it goes through an ADM and onto our third network topology, a ring. Telecom networks are susceptible to failure from all sorts of sources, whether it be from construction work and a backhoe cutting through the fiber, from rodents eating through the fiber, or from human error or any of a myriad of other causes. One major reason for these cuts is that the fibers are buried in the same right-of-ways as other utilities like water or gas pipes. Rings provide a high degree of protection with nominal reserved bandwidth. Let's take a look at these restoration schemes to get an appreciation for SONET rings.

In understanding automatic protection switching (APS), there are three factors to consider. First, there's the issue of speed of the switchover. SONET can switch

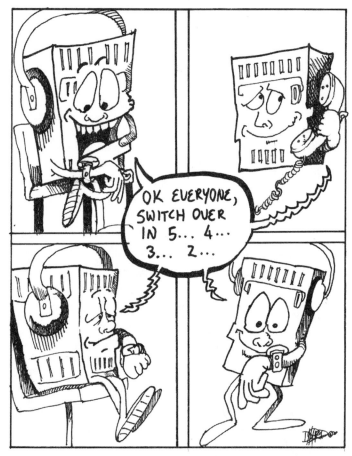

UNBEKNOWNST TO THE ENGINEERS, SONET
SWITCHES DEVELOP THEIR OWN FAILOVER MECHANISM.

around a failure within 50 milliseconds, fast enough that higher-layer protocols, like IP, would never see the hiccup. Yet this is possible only if capacity has been reserved for the task. This brings up the second issue—cost. To underutilize fiber for the one time that restoration is needed is a terribly inefficient use of a valuable resource. This has led to alternative restoration schemes where carriers look at reserving some amount of capacity as a backup of a much large channel—kind of like relying on ISDN backup for a leased line.

There's one other issue to think through, particularly when changing restoration schemes in existing installations: the direction of the fiber ducting. Depending on how the ducts run, fiber topologies might be very limited. Rings are often the only feasible network topology within the metro, because that's how the fibers run. Alternative schemes would require installing new fiber ducting, significantly increasing the cost of deployment.

The simplest protection scheme protects a line with another line. So-called one-for-one (1:1) schemes can recover from any single fiber cut, but they require allocating spare capacity equivalent to the used capacity, which isn't particularly efficient, particularly since the spare capacity can't be used for carrying any traffic. More efficient is 1:N protection, where one line protects up to 14 lines, This scheme, besides using less capacity, also allows carrying traffic on the spare line.

Rings, on the other hand, can offer effective restoration with lower capacity requirements. SONET specifies two general types of rings: UPSR (unidirectional path-switched rings) and BLSR (bidirectional line-switched rings). With UPSR, a backup ring sits idle, and when there's a failure, ADMs jump to the next ring. BLSR can use the backup ring for data, which is bumped in the event of a failure. A 4F-BLSR ring uses four fibers, two in each direction, offering dedicated protection with alternative ring path and span protection. A 2F-BLSR ring uses two fibers, one in each direction, and offers dedicated protection with an alternative ring path (see Figure 7.3).

SONET Service Mappings

We might think of these configurations as the solid lines that appear in the diagram, but in reality they are much more complex. Under SONET, the communication between the two offices would be described as a path composed of a series of lines and sections (see Figure 7.4).

At the most abstract there's the **path**. Think of the path as the connection between the two offices. Of course, since we're speaking SONET, the path only runs from where SONET begins, and it ends at the edges of the providers' networks. The T1 lines that attach the customer's headquarters and remote office to the public network are not part of the SONET network and hence are not in the path.

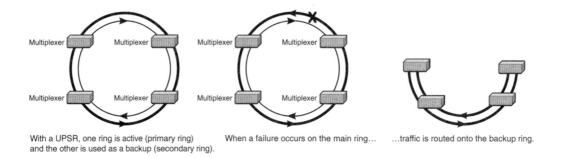

With a UPSR, one ring is active (primary ring) and the other is used as a backup (secondary ring).

When a failure occurs on the main ring…

…traffic is routed onto the backup ring.

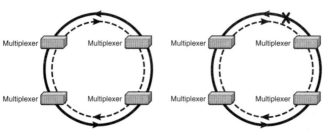

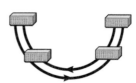

With a BLSR, the primary ring carries high-priority traffic and the secondary ring is used to carry lower-priority traffic, for example.

When a failure occurs on the primary ring…

…high-priority traffic is routed onto the backup ring while low-priority traffic is either dropped or sent as well.

Figure 7.3
Two types of SONET rings.

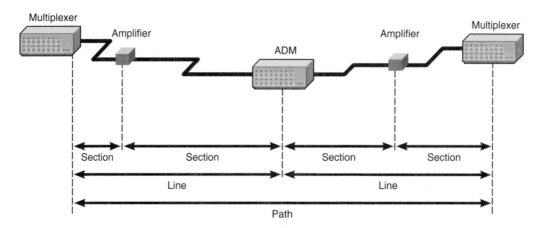

Figure 7.4
SONET service mappings.

This path, though, is really just a virtual construct. Underneath it is the physical line that runs between the network elements. Each **line**, though, likely consists of multiple copper or fiber sections linked by amplifiers or regenerators to boost the signals. Each portion of the line is called a **section**. Keep these three terms in mind—paths, lines, and sections—as they'll become particularly important when we look at SONET framing.

SONET Framing

Now that we've looked at SONET's hierarchy and architecture, we can better understand its guts—the SONET framing structure. SONET is known especially for its ability to deliver low-level network management information. A brief glance at a SONET frame makes it easy to see why. Though it is about half the size of an Ethernet frame (810 bytes vs. 1518 bytes), it contains about 100 percent more management information.

The frame itself is depicted as a segmented rectangle 90 columns wide by 9 rows deep. Don't be fooled—it's still delivered as a single stream of bits. The frame is sent from left to right, top to bottom (see Figure 7.5).

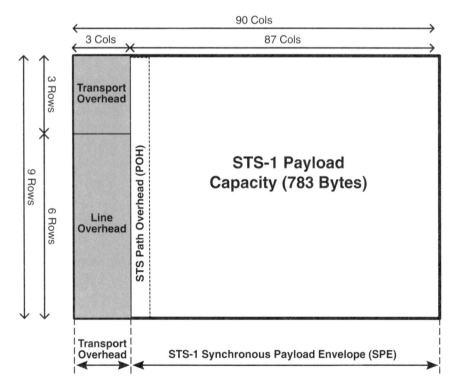

Figure 7.5
Simplified depiction of an STS-1 frame.

Here's the score. As an STS-1 frame travels down the wire, its components get read and stripped out at different points, what we'll call stages. Stage one is the regenerator that designates the end of a section (we told you those terms would come in handy). Stage two is, pardon the pun, at the end of a line and stage three is, you guessed it, the end of the path, the final SONET destination.

So it shouldn't be surprising that the structure of the SONET frame reflects these different network components. It has four sections. Three of them contain information overhead for doing network management and fault identification on section, lines, and paths, and the fourth contains the actual data of the **SONET payload**. The first three columns contain the section overhead (the first three lines) and the line overhead (the last six lines). Together the two are called the transport overhead. The last 87 columns contain the path overhead (the first column) and the payload, together called the SONET payload envelope (SPE). For synchronization issues, an SPE will span successive frames.

As you start concatenating these STS-1 frames together to form STS-3cs, the frame structure gets trickier. The transport overheads are consolidated at the front of the frame and the SPEs at the back of the frame (see Figure 7.6).

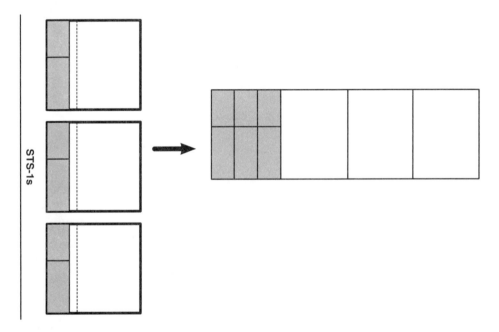

Figure 7.6
Simplified depiction of an STS-3c frame.

Smaller granularities are accommodated by stuffing the SPE frames with concatenated VTs. Each type of VT is kept in a separate group, with up to seven VT groups in an STS-1. Each group can contain either VT1.5s, VT2s, VT3s, or a VT6. Thus, below STS-1 speeds customers can scale their networks in 1.5 increments, albeit with a lot more complexity. Above STS-1 speeds, networks grow in STS-1 increments.

SONET Challenges

The good news is that SONET is a dramatic improvement over async and PDH communications. Even today SONET remains excellent at delivering very reliable and highly predictable services, like voice. Anyone who's been involved in the PC world, where technology churn can occur every three to six months, has to be amazed at a technology that's lasted for nearly 20 years. If not for the radical changes in traffic types, SONET would probably continue along for another decade or so. But telecommunications *is* changing, and though the voice constitutes the majority of revenue-generating traffic, the huge growth of traffic overall is coming from data. Providers are starting to look at ways of retaining the merits of SONET—the reliability, predictability, and manageability of the protocol—while addressing six limitations:

1. **Limited flexibility**—SONET is still limited in its ability to dish up lines of different speed. Most SONET gear still does not support VT concatenation, so customers who want a 10 Mbits/s connection need an STS-1 link. Even when VT concatenation is offered, speeds above STS-1 grow in very fat increments. So a customer who wants 70 Mbits/s can end up purchasing 100 Mbits/s (two times STS-1). Realistically, though, often only an OC-3 (155 Mbits/s) is offered by the carrier.

2. **Inefficiencies**—With their fixed payloads, SONET frames are fine for carrying voice, but data is another matter. Traditionally, mapping Ethernet frames onto SONET frames often means underutilizing the network, as portions of time slots are left unused. Even on voice calls, though, SONET uses more capacity than necessary. Think about how much time is spent during a conversation actually speaking. Typically, there are pauses or breaks or times when one person listens and the other speaks. These pauses represent potential bandwidth savings that some estimates put at up to 50 percent of a normal telephone conversation.

3. **Lots of equipment**—One big benefit of SONET is that it lets us extract time slots without having to demux the entire signal. Even so, SONET requires a substantial amount of gear to be located at the carrier's premises. Customers need to install an add-drop multiplexer to get on and off the core network. A DCS is needed to direct the specific channels around, and then multiplexers are needed to recombine the signals. This

doesn't even include the networking gear for supporting voice, IP, and private data services or the expertise for running them.

4. **Slow provisioning**—Ordering a circuit today can take three to four weeks to process. SONET pundits point out that the equipment could be configured, or provisioned as it's called in the industry, within minutes. The real problem lies in the bureaucracy associated with the provisioning. However, that also assumes that customers need to be attached to the SONET network, which typically is not the case. Finding a way to reduce the provisioning time regardless of whether customers are located on copper or fiber connections is increasingly critical.

5. **Limited flexibility**—When an OC-3/STM-1 channel is established between two points, there are actually two channels created, one for receiving and one for receiving in the same speed and direction. The problem is that much Internet traffic remains asymmetrical, again wasting bandwidth. Similarly, if streaming media become the predominant type of data on the Internet, there must be an effective way for one station, the broadcaster, to send video to other stations, the consumers. There is no construct in SONET for providing this type of communication.

The SONET Answer

These developments have forced SONET pundits to adapt the technology to the changing times. A new set of protocols will be better suited for carrying corporate data. The generic framing protocol (GFP, g.gfp) for the first time provides a standard measure for packing nonvoice traffic into a SONET frame, enabling compliant equipment from different manufacturers to share data over SONET. With virtual concatenation, intermediate steps which weren't previously defined, like STS-2, now become possible. This would enable a carrier to transport an Ethernet signal, for example, more efficiently than if an STS-3 were required. Another protocol, the link capacity adjustment scheme (LCAS), enables the bandwidth of these links to be increased or decreased without interrupting the traffic flow.

Finally, the T1 XI committee is taking two steps to improve SONET's top performance. The ratified OC-768 specification paves the way for vendors to implement 40 Gbits/s interfaces on their equipment. At the same time, a new proposal looks to improve SONET scalability by enabling SONET to span multiple wavelengths.

Beyond SONET

Still, as SONET pundits look to adjust the protocol for the twenty-first century, others see the opportunity to address these challenges by creating entirely new technologies.

Some technologies are emerging with the same synchronous orientation that SONET has popularized. Others are adapting more of the LAN technologies used in corporate offices. We'll start looking at these different approaches in the next chapter.

SHORT CUTS...

SONET is very effective at delivering predictable traffic requiring predictable access to the network. The technology is less well suited to carrying corporate data traffic with its bursty traffic patterns.

SONET uses a single clock to neatly combine time slots together. Previous technologies used multiple clocks, making them less effective at dividing the available bandwidth.

SONET works on a hierarchy of signals. The smallest channel increments are the virtual tributaries (VTs), which are combined into synchronous transport signals (STSs) for electrical interfaces and optical carrier (OC) for optical interfaces.

There are four sections to the SONET frame—three carrying information overhead for doing network management and fault identification on section, lines, and paths, and the fourth carrying the actual data, called the SONET payload.

The first three columns of the SONET frame contain the section overhead (the first three lines) and the line overhead (the last six lines). Together the two are called the transport overhead. The last 87 columns contain the path over head (the first column) and the payload, called together the SONET payload Envelope (SPE).

The traditional SONET environment suffers from five major problems: limited flexibility, lots of equipment, slow provisioning, support for only bidirectional traffic, and no support for point-to-multipoint traffic.

8 Metro Core Technologies

In this chapter...

WHEN SALES TAKE OVER THE LAB

FRUSTRATED WITH HAVING TO DEAL WITH ENGINEERS, MARKETERS RE-INVENT THE METRO NETWORK.

Nowhere is the challenge of optical revolution more significant than in the metropolitan-area networks. While developments in DWDM long ago (as in about two to three years ago) revolutionized the long haul network by providing the huge amounts of capacity they require, that's not the case for the more price-sensitive, highly competitive metro networks.

The combination of metro's requirements are unique, blending aspects of the long-haul and, as we'll see later, the access networks. Capacities in the metro core aren't quite as large as in the long-haul, but are significantly more than in the access. Whereas the long haul network providers think in terms of 10 Gbits/s links with an eye toward 40 Gbits/s over hundreds and thousands of kilometers, metro providers typically think in terms of 2.5 Gbits/s topping out at 10 Gbits/s spanning tens or low-hundreds of kilometers. Utilizing fibers more efficiently is a big concern, but there are other issues as well, such as handling the different types of traffic traveling over the network, congestion management and control, and the like.

Numerous technologies are looking to address the problem. WDM is making its way into metro. **Dynamic transfer mode (DTM)** is a standard in the SONET mode from the **European Telecommunications Standards Institute (ETSI)** and is particularly adapted to carrying video traffic. On the other hand, the packet pundits are pushing two: 10 Gigabit Ethernet (10GE) and a new protocol called **resilient packet ring (RPR)** as a kind of generic transport for all types of services. Over the longer term, the real successor may lie in the **optical transport network (OTN)**, which will define a new switched hierarchy for very large pipes.

The New Metro

There are two components to the metro solution: the boxes that sit in the central office connecting to the public network and the transmission technology running the network itself. Today's central offices are a cornucopia of technologies. Along with the SONET

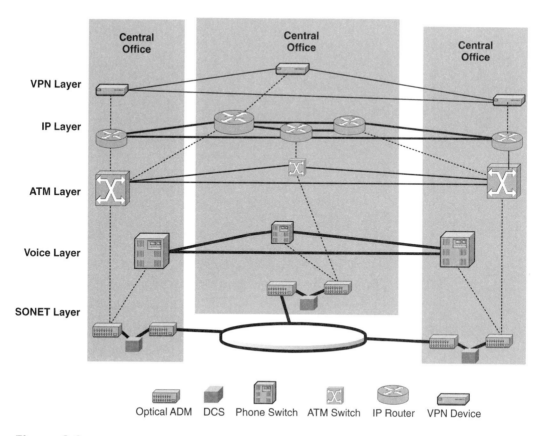

Figure 8.1
Today's central offices consist of different layers, each requiring its own equipment.

equipment, each service offered by the provider requires its own equipment. Internet services demand routers and switches and must be installed. If additional high-level IP services are also being provided, like managed firewall or VPN services, then more equipment is required. Similarly, private data services today can use frame relay and ATM, each of which may require its own switches and interfaces (see Figure 8.1).

The problem with all of this equipment is multifold. Each device takes a certain level of physical facilities to maintain. Power must be supplied. Physical room must be found to house the different boxes. What's more, the new technologies bring their own inherent complexity, requiring additional expertise, not to mention network management complexity. Today provisioning an IP connection between locations could mean configuring three sets of equipment—IP, frame relay or ATM, and SONET—increasing the cost and the time needed to deliver a service.

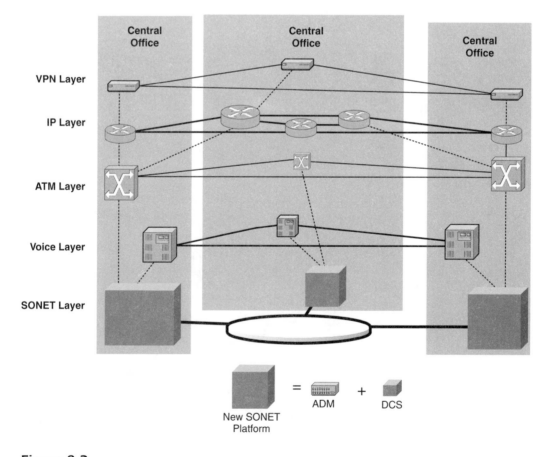

Figure 8.2
The new metro networks combine optical ADMs and DCS functions into a single box.

Providers would like to find a way to cut those costs by minimizing the technologies deployed and the boxes installed. Vendors have responded with a number of integrated devices. Some consolidate core SONET functionality, like DCS and ADMs (see Figure 8.2).

Others go even further and create a kind of optical Swiss army knife, at times called a "**God-Box**," combining optical switching, ATM and/or frame relay switching, IP routing, add-drop multiplexing, and DWDM, for example, into a single unit (see Figure 8.3).

These approaches certainly reduce box count, but they are not without potential drawbacks. Carriers have very diverse requirements, which can't always be easily addressed by a single box. What's more, by developing multiple functions in a box instead of specializing, providers run the risk of not being able to deliver the best of any function.

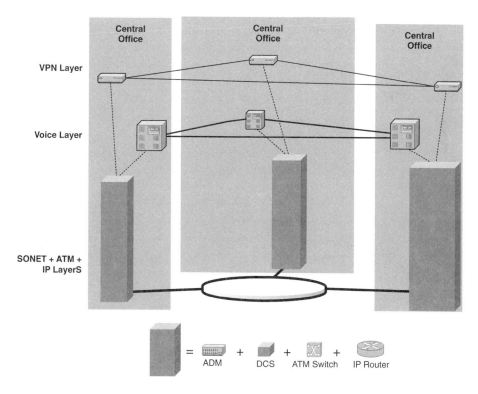

Figure 8.3
So-called "God-Boxes" combine ADM and DCS functionality as well as ATM switching and IP routing into a single box.

The Technologies

Another way to eliminate costs is by reducing the number of networks needed to deliver a service. Instead of running IP over frame relay over SONET over optics, for example, just run IP over optics. The spread of IP has led metro solutions providers to split into two basic camps. There are those that lean toward creating discrete networks for different services and those that advocate putting all services over IP.

Let's start with the proponents of different networks. Here there are basically three approaches: metro-WDM solutions, DTM, and OTN. Metro-WDM solutions look to adapt long-haul technology to the shorter reaches of the metropolitan network. By reducing the channel count and the distances, and in particular the lasers, less expensive components can be used, reducing system costs.

With DWDM, the metro core no longer consists of one wavelength segmented by SONET, but of individual wavelengths. This gives carriers large amounts of capacity and flexibility in provisioning their networks. Since the bandwidth is "clear"—that is, there's no underlying protocol shaping the characteristics of the network—any type of traffic can be provided over a wavelength without necessarily wasting bandwidth or sacrificing service quality. One wavelength can be devoted to carrying voice traffic, for example, and another wavelength to carrying data traffic (see Figure 8.4).

Finally, by integrating multiple devices together, Metro DWDM systems significantly simplify deployment. Instead of having to provision an underlying physical layer, a SONET layer, and an IP layer, all services are provisioned once through a common protocol, like **generalized multiprotocol label switching** (GMPLS, see Chapter 10).

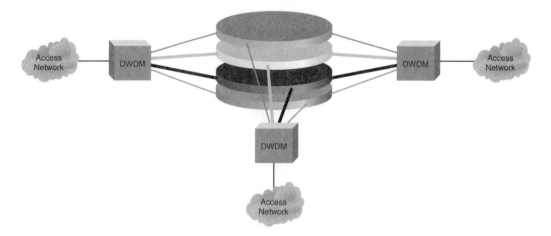

Figure 8.4
Metro DWDM systems use different wavelengths to carry different types of traffic, depending on carrier requirements.

DTM

While Metro DWDM technologies provide plenty of capacity, costs have traditionally been quite high. Other technologies have emerged to address single-wavelength networks or to run over the individual wavelength in a multiwavelength system. These technologies are DTM, 10 Gigabits/s Ethernet, and RPR, each optimized for slightly different applications (see Figure 8.5).

Some proponents maintain that with video emerging as the primary traffic generator of the future, the network should be video optimized. Dynamic synchronous transfer mode (DTM) aims to do just that. The protocol seeks to address SONET's limitations without sacrificing the benefits of quality of service offered in a synchronous data stream.

Advocates of DTM argue that to address these issues we need a new synchronous transport. DTM aims to provide the guaranteed service quality of SONET with more flexible channel configurations than SONET.

The DTM network consists of switches configured in the same range of topologies as SONET—point to point, hub, or ring. The network runs at 1 gigabit/s and is divided into 8000 frames/s, or a frame every 125 microseconds (µs). Each frame consists of 64-bit time slots with 1950 time slots per frame for a total of 512 Kbits/s per slot.

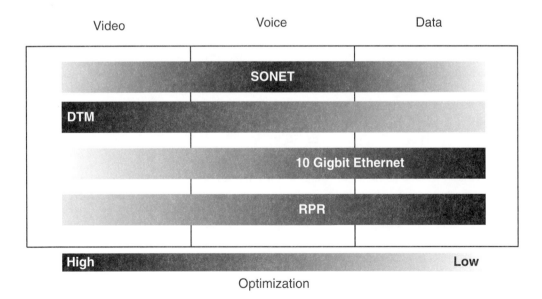

Figure 8.5
Metro technology optimization points.

Five protocols are used in DTM to minimize manual configuration of the network and simplify network management. These protocols are the DTM channel protocol (DCP) for establishing a channel, DTM resource management protocol (DRMP) for changing the size of a channel, DTM routing protocol (DRP) for topology discovery, DTM link state protocol (DLSP) for identifying the optimum path through the network, and DTM synchronization protocol (DSYP) for maintaining synchronization between equipment. A sixth, DTM physical protocol (DPP), determines how information is physically sent onto the DTM network.

When DTM switches receive information to put onto the network, they initiate channel setup using DCP. DCP is also used to tear down or change the characteristics of the channel. These characteristics might cover the number of time slots allocated to a given channel as well as the type of traffic that the channel will support.

With the channel set up, the switch is ready to start transmitting. The structure of the bits is handled by DPP. The protocol today defines two formats—DPP-8B10B when running over optics directly and DPP-VC4 when running over SONET. The latter might sound somewhat strange, as then you have a synchronous network operating within another synchronous network.

In reality this will be quite common, as providers who are interested in DTM will likely have SONET already installed. Providing the means for running over SONET enables them to channelize their bandwidth with the flexibility of DTM without the cost of upgrading and changing over an entire network. DPP-VC4 interfaces are being developed for STM-1 (51.9 Mbits/s), STM-16 (2.5 Gbits/s), and STM-64 (10 Gbits/s).

So now the channel is established and the network is operating, but what happens when network conditions change—if a line is cut, for example, or if there's congestion on the network? DCP can change the characteristics of the channel, but it can't alter the network resources themselves. To do that you need DRMP. Switches handle the resources on the network, and DRMP makes routing decisions as to where to send frames destined for another network, manages resources, and enables switches to reuse time slots through a process called scooping.

This last point is extremely significant. With slot reuse, switches on a network can move time slots between interfaces to avoid bottlenecks. DCP also insures that links between nodes remain utilized in a technology called spatial reuse. Unlike SONET, where the two nodes connected through a channel use up that channel for the entire network, spatial reuse enables different pairs of nodes to communicate with each other over the same time slot, presuming that conversation is only between those devices (see Figure 8.6).

And how do those stations maintain the accuracy of those time slots? Through DTM's synchronization protocol (DSYP). Like SONET, DTM uses a single clock, off which all the other nodes in the network work. DSYP establishes and maintains this synchronization in the case of network faults.

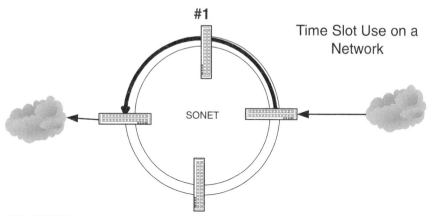

With SONET, a time-slot used for communicating between two nodes can only be used for those two nodes on any part of the network.

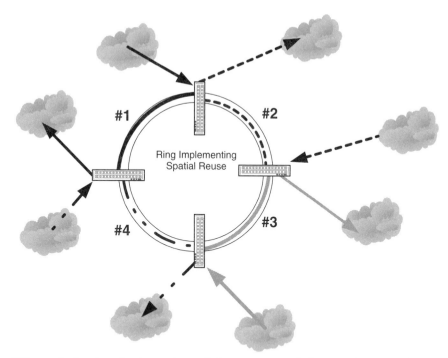

When a technology implements spatial reuse, unused slots can be reused for transmission between devices, in this case four times the number of transmissions at the same time.

Figure 8.6
Spatial reuse explained.

DLSP simplifies device setup and installation through autodetection. Install a new device on a corporate network and the device will often announce its presence to all other nodes on the network. There's no need to run around from station to station configuring different vendors' equipment with the address of the new station. It all happens automatically. The same goes for DTM. DTM switches will automatically detect new devices using the DLSP algorithms. The same algorithm will enable them to detect the network topology and any changes or failures in that topology.

DSLP also gives DTM its redundancy. Like SONET rings, DTM rings are two types of *network* redundancy. Should a switch on a DTM network fail, the adjacent nodes will isolate the failure and wrap around a protection ring. Similarly, if a link should fail, the adjacent devices isolate the link.

10 GIGABIT ETHERNET ....

Data networking pundits believe a network can be developed that's equally adept at handling real-time streaming video as well as non-time-sensitive protocols, such as Web browsing and email. Their solution is a combination of Ethernet, IP, and MPLS.

The presence of IP is not surprising. The protocol runs the Internet today. Ethernet is another matter. The access method that dominates in the corporate network, at first glance it lacks the key characteristics needed to be adopted in the WAN. There are no management facilities for troubleshooting built into the protocol. Ability to guarantee quality of service is questionable, and a top speed of 1 Gbit/s is just fast enough for the public network.

All of these are good reasons for the standards group who invented Ethernet to develop 10 Gbits/s Ethernet, dubbed **802.3ae**. The protocol addresses many of these very problems and brings something for which Ethernet is well known: low cost. Although it's still early, the common belief is that with Ethernet's huge market presence in the corporate network, Ethernet products will be dramatically cheaper than other solutions. There's good reason to believe such reasoning. Aside from the cost benefits of mass production, Ethernet products won't have to carry the additional costs of converting between protocols or network infrastructure solutions. An Ethernet router connecting into the public network will be able to have Ethernet on either side without having to pay for SONET, DTM, or RPR interfaces.

Like the rest of the Ethernet standards, 10GigE uses the same basic frame formatting of the original 10 Mbits/s specification. As such, it becomes fairly easy to connect 10GigE networks with 10 and 100 Mbits/s and 1 Gbits/s Ethernet networks (see Figure 2.10). 10GE will also use only the duplex mode operation of 1 Gbit/s. With duplex operation, stations send and receive data on two channels. There are no collisions, so there's no need for the CSMA/CD algorithm.

Where 10 Gbits/s differs most is in the physical layer, which Ethernet divides into the physical media dependent (PMD) and physical coding sublayer (PCS). The standards group defined two PHYs—a LAN PHY (10GBase-R) and a WAN PHY (10GBase-W or 10GBase-X). The WAN PHY has all the functionality of the LAN PHY plus management information specific to the WAN. The difference between them is in the PCS (see Figure 8.7).

It's important to realize the perspective here of the 10GE Ethernet community. The creation of a WAN PHY is in many ways a less than perfect situation—a nod to the market, which today is dominated by SONET. With the WAN PHY, Ethernet traffic is packed into SONET frames for transport across a SONET network. However, as the protocol evolves, Ethernet vendors believe that the protocol will extend into the WAN. Ultimately, the public network will become a large LAN, if you will, running the Ethernet LAN PHY.

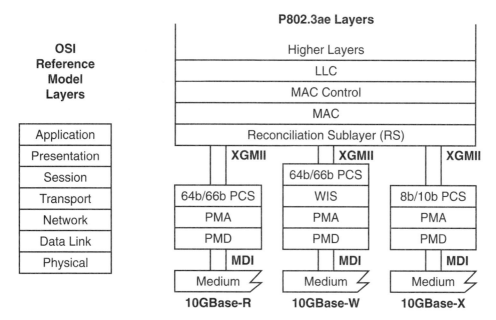

MDI = Medium Dependent Interface
XGMII = 10-Gigabit Media Independent Interface
PCS = Physical Coding Sublayer
PMA = Physical Medium Attachment
PMD = Physical Medium Dependent
WIS = WAN Interface Sublayer

Figure 8.7
The 10 Gbits/s Ethernet standards group defined three types of physical interfaces: 10GBase-R for single-wavelength LAN connections, 10GBase-W for WAN connections, and 10GBase-X for multiwavelength systems. The difference between Base-R and Base-W lies in the WIS sublayer that provides SONET Frame (Source: 10 Gigabit Ethernet Alliance).

To enable this to happen, the 802.3ae group has isolated the differences between the two PHYs to specific components that can be swapped out when necessary. Both the WAN and LAN PHYs run over the same fiber options. The group specified five fiber types—two for multimode and three for single-mode (see Table 8.1).

The differences lie in the PCS. Both the Serial LAN and WAN PHY use the same encoding scheme—64B66B. The WWDM implementation can use the 8B10B encoding scheme specified for 1 Gbit/s Ethernet. The differences between the two serial interfaces is in the WAN's additional sublayer called the WAN interface sublayer (WIS) (see Figure 8.8). WIS provides the simplified SONET framer and adjusts the PHYs output to work at 9.953 Gbits/s, the speed of a SONET OC-192/STM-64 network and not the 10.3 Gbits/s used by 10GE.

Table 8.1   Fiber Choices for 10 Gbits/s Ethernet

PMD (Optical Transceiver)	Type of Fiber Supported	Target Distance (Meters)
850 nm serial	Multimode	65
1310 nm WWDM*	Multimode	300
1310 nm WWDM	Single-mode	10,000
1310 nm serial	Single-mode	10,000
1550 nm serial	Single-mode	40,000

WWDM = wide wave-division multiplexing

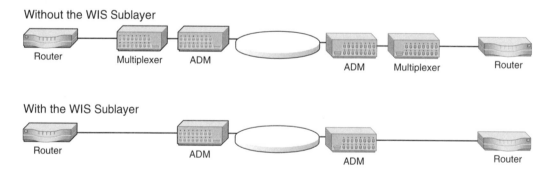

Figure 8.8
By adding the WIS sublayer, routers can connect directly to the SONET network with 10 Gbits/s Ethernet, saving the cost and complexity of an additional multiplexer and providing a migration path to an all-Ethernet network.

This doesn't make Ethernet a WAN technology. It simply allows Ethernet to be easily transported across a SONET network. Now two routers can be attached directly to a SONET network instead of having to go through a multiplexer (see Figure 8.8).

To enable this transition easily, 10 GB created something called the XAUI (pronounced Zowie) interface. XAUI or X (as in the Roman numeral 10) attachment unit interface (AUI) is a high-speed bus that runs on four lanes clocking at 2.5 times the speed of 1 Gbit/s Ethernet. Using just four data paths, and not dozens of lower-speed paths, simplifies board layout, but at the same time can't connect to the lower-speed, lower-costing Ethernet MAC chips. To make this connection possible, the 10 GB working group developed the **XGMII** interface, a lower-costing, 32-bit data path that's then converted into the high-speed **XAUI** bus (see Figure 8.9).

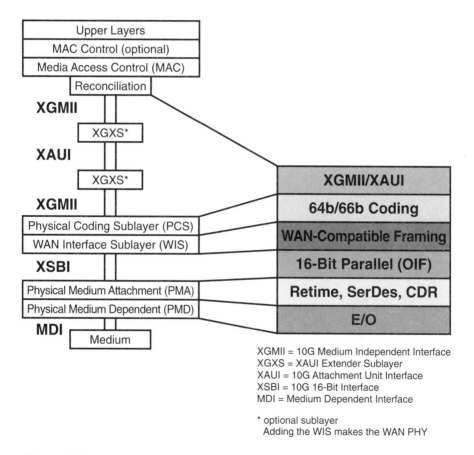

XGMII = 10G Medium Independent Interface
XGXS = XAUI Extender Sublayer
XAUI = 10G Attachment Unit Interface
XSBI = 10G 16-Bit Interface
MDI = Medium Dependent Interface

* optional sublayer
  Adding the WIS makes the WAN PHY

Figure 8.9
Through XGMII and XAUI existing, Ethernet MAC chips can be used in building a 10 Gbits/s Ethernet interface (Source: 10 Gigabit Ethernet Alliance).

CHALLENGES FOR 10 GIG ....

While 10 Gbits/s Ethernet offers significant amounts of bandwidth and is well suited to carrying data, there are two major challenges.

The first big problem facing 10 Gig adoption lies in the physical architecture. Today's metro fiber networks are wired in rings. Practically, ring architectures are useful because the number of trenches that need to be built to carry the fiber is nominal as compared to a mesh of point-to-point links. Ethernet, however, does not inherently support a ring architecture. If the 10GigE then is wired, either upstream or downstream nodes, depending on the network configuration, will have preferred access to the network (see Figure 8.10).

Another problem lies in the QoS support. The QoS method used in 802 provides for labeling of traffic, but no policing of the traffic once on the ring. Implementations involving IP QoS and multiprotocol label switching (MPLS) are more robust, though there are concerns that even with those schemes problems might exist as lines become heavily loaded. We'll learn more about MPLS in Chapter 10.

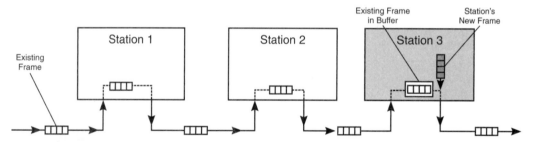

When Ethernet is configured as a network of point-to-point links, the last station can have an unfair advantage by buffering the existing network frame and having free access to the ring.

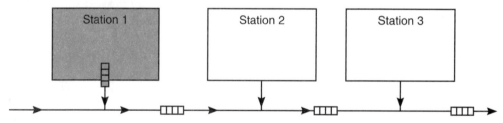

When Ethernet is configured as a shared medium, Station 1 has the advantage because it is the first to see a clear link.

Figure 8.10
Upstream-downstream fairness problems on Ethernet rings.

Similarly there's the problem of fault protection. Today Ethernet doesn't have a scheme for instant fail-over. Typically that's not a problem, since Ethernet networks are wired as a full mesh where data can be routed around failures in the line. However, the router convergence needed to do that kind of rerouting can take several seconds, far too long for today's public networks. To some extent this is expected to be addressed by MPLS, though today that MPLS feature is not yet standardized.

RPR

Largely as a result of these concerns, providers started developing a new protocol better suited toward ring architectures. The protocol, called resilient packet ring (RPR), comes from the IEEE 802.17 working group. The standard largely grew out of some technology by Cisco Systems, Inc., called **spatial reuse protocol (SRP)** and branded as **dynamic packet transport (DPT)**. It's also referred to in the industry as "optical Ethernet," though it has little to do with Ethernet beyond having an Ethernet port sitting on an RPR box.

What RPR does is three things, all referred to in its name. *Resilient* refers to the protocol's ability to work around failures by using at least two counterrotating rings simultaneously, similar to DTM. Should one fail, then the RPR nodes will jump to the backup ring and continue operation. Also like DTM, RPR uses **spatial reuse technology**, so bandwidth isn't "pinned up" across these rings. Rather, capacity used for one transmission in one part of the network can be reused for another transmission in another part of network, provided they don't interfere with one another (see Figure 8.5).

The technology is based around frames or *packets*, hence the term. Unlike Ethernet, though, RPR offers three levels of built-in quality of service. The synchronous traffic class (STC) will enable providers to run high-quality voice traffic, for example, over RPR. With guaranteed traffic class (GTC), providers will be able to deliver a high-quality data service where they commit to a specified level of service. The third class, the best effort traffic class (BETC), will be used for a data service with no specific guarantees.

The exact functioning of the protocol is a matter of some debate. Some proponents argue that RPR nodes should not be aware of the available capacity on the networks. Rather, they take incoming Ethernet packets, for example, on one side and pack them into an RPR frame. The frame gets labeled with a particular traffic priority and then goes onto the network. The frame transits across the ring, where its destination address and priority are inspected by each node on the network. When the frame reaches its final destination, the station removes the transit frame from the ring for delivery to the next destination.

The only exception to this last point is in the case of **multicast** traffic. Multicasting is a way of sending one frame to multiple recipients. With a multicast frame, both approaches call for the transmitting station to remove the frame from the network.

Simple, right? But what happens if a station has two frames to send—the transit frame and the RPR station's own frame, the transmit frame? To handle such a case, each RPR node is equipped with high-priority and low-priority transit buffers. After stations check the transit frame's address and decide the frame should not be removed from the network, the frame is placed into the appropriate transit queue. High-priority transit frames then are serviced first, followed by high-priority transmit frames. Low-priority transit and transmit frames are serviced through a fair-queuing algorithm giving them equal access to the network.

If the low-priority transit queues start to back up, then the switch signals to other stations to throttle back their transmissions. The queue is cleared and, after a predetermined period of time, the stations start to increase the speed of their transmissions again (see Figure 8.11).

The alternative approach shuns the use of this rather large buffer. Under this model, the nodes are aware of available capacity on the network. Once the frame is received and the address inspected, it is put into a transit buffer for transmission on the ring. This time the transit buffer is much shorter, the size of the maximum-sized RPR frame. If the node has another frame to send, the transiting frame wins out. If this happens too many times and the transmitting frames within the RPR node can't be sent, the switches signal upstream (or downstream) to the other nodes to reconfigure access to the network to enable the higher-priority frame to be sent (see Figure 8.12).

The division within the RPR ranks could create significant troubles for the technology. This is particularly true given the competition—Ethernet. Although Ethernet may not be targeted at ring networks, like RPR, Ethernet is competing for the metro core. The protocol's ease of use and low cost were sufficient to defeat Token Ring and ATM in the corporate network. While factors such as the lack of QoS will hinder Ethernet's deployment within the Metro, the protocol will prove to be a formidable competitor to RPR.

OTN

As data pundits have looked at replacing SONET with their new protocols, so too have the ITU and ANSI, under whose tutelage the SONET has developed, formed a SONET successor. The new protocol, the optical transport hierarchy (OTN), is meant to replace SONET as the solution for building very high bandwidth, public network transports.

There are two levels to consider in OTN: the transport layer, and the signaling and management layer. Both aim to address fundamental problems that remain in SONET. The biggest is capacity. By now it should be clear that SONET is starting to run out of gas. Despite the improvements in WDM technology, SONET still remains a single-wavelength solution. There is no simple way to aggregate multiple wavelengths,

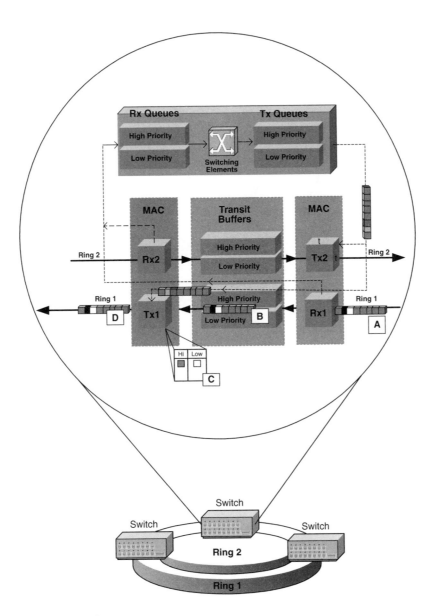

Figure 8.11

With the first approach, as a packet enters an RPR node on one ring (Ring 1), an address lookup is performed (A). If the packet is not meant for the node, it's placed in a transit buffer (B) for retransmission onto the network. If another frame needs to be sent at the same time, the priorities of both frames are compared (C). The one with the highest priority is sent first (D). Should a failure occur, the network switches over to the backup ring that operates in the same way.

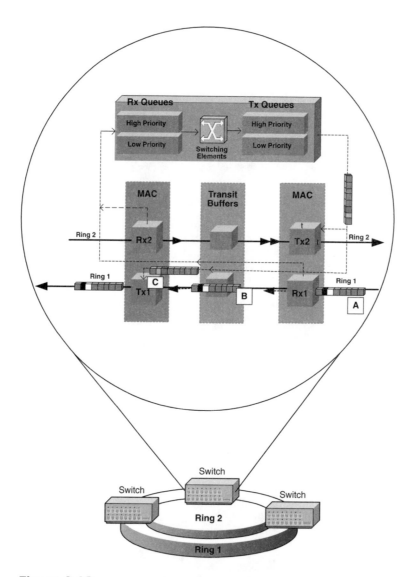

Figure 8.12

With the second approach, a much smaller transit buffer, just the size of one frame, is used. The frame enters an RPR node on one ring (Ring 1), and an address look-up is performed (A). If the packet is not meant for the node, it's placed in a transit buffer (B) for retransmission onto the network. If another frame needs to be sent at the same time, the transit frame takes precedence (C). If the node can't send its frame, then it signals to the other nodes on the network to reconfigure the network to give it access in order to throttle back transmission. Should a failure occur, the network switches over to the backup ring that operates in the same way.

or for that matter fibers, together to increase capacity between locations. What this means is that providers are left managing two layers—the SONET network as well as series of point-to-point WDM circuits—a very complex task indeed. What they'd like to get to is a point where the intricacies of the WDM connections are masked from the upper layers and they are simply treated as one seamless network. SONET can't help on that point.

What's more, there's a big problem with efficiencies at higher capacities. SONET hierarchy isn't optimized for large data transfers. As the hierarchy gets concatenated up to larger chunks of capacity, more overhead is needed for handling SONET management information.

As work began on addressing those two points, other issues—most notably SONET's implementation of tandem connection monitoring—also became a hot point. Today SONET provides a mechanism for monitoring tandem connections, but those capabilities were added rather late to SONET. Networkers were looking at ways of providing more information from the outset with OTN.

OTN Transport

OTN has a number of similarities to SONET. Its connections are divided into three components, and there's a hierarchy for how data can be combined together. Yet, aside from those very gross similarities, the protocols are fundamentally different. SONET assumes a synchronous architecture working off a single fiber. OTN is fundamentally an asynchronous medium made up of point-to-point optical links

Let's start with the similarities. Like SONET, OTN divides connections down into three components, four if you count the fiber. With SONET those components were the path (the logical connection between stations), the line (the underlying physical link), and the sections (the individual copper or fiber spans terminating at amplifiers or regenerators that together formed the link).

OTN's structure is similar, though divided differently, because it accounts for the deployment of WDM. The OTN elements are optical channels, optical multiplex sections, and optical transmission sections. At each layer, connections between two end points called trails contain data from the layer above as well as management information for terminating and troubleshooting the trail. The troubleshooting services provide the ability to check for the presence of a connection at the particular layer, inspect the quality of transmission, and detect problems if there are any.

Optical channel connection, or trails as they're called, are conceptually similar to the SONET path with the goal of providing end-to-end networking. The optical channel layer (OCh) transports client signals between two end points on the OTN.

Optical multiplex sections (OMSs) describe the WDM portions that underpin these optical channels. These are similar to SONET lines, but they account for the use of multiple wavelengths, of which SONET is ignorant. As such, optical multiplex section data streams consist of some number of optical channels aggregated together. The result is that the optical channel sees one fat pipe and not several small pipes. Each channel has a defined frequency and optical bandwidth and can be indicated as being in or out of service.

At the bottom of the OTN link is the optical transmission section (OTS). Like SONET links, OTSs provide for transmission of signals over individual fiber spans. The OTS defines a physical interface detailing optical parameters such as frequency, power level, and signal-to-noise ratio.

OTN Hierarchy

Like SONET, OTN defines a network hierarchy called the optical transport hierarchy (OTH). Just as SONET is built on STS-1 increments that can be concatenated together to build larger connections, so too OTH is built on a base unit, the optical transport module (OTM) increment.

But here's the big difference—OTMs can span multiple wavelengths and each wavelength can be composed of links operating at different speed. To indicate this difference OTMs carry two suffixes, n and m, written as OTM-$n.m$, where n refers to the maximum number of wavelengths supported at the lowest bit rate on the wavelength while m indicates the bit rate supported on the interface. Three speeds are supported: 2.5 Bits/s indicated by a 1, 10 Bits/s indicated by a 2, and 40 Bits/s indicated by a 3, but an interface might support some combination of them—namely, 2.5 and 10 Bits/s (1 and 2), 10 Bits/s and 40 (2 and 3) Bits/s, or all three (1, 2, and 3). Thus an OTM-3.2 would indicate an OTM that spans three wavelengths, each operating at least at 10 Gbits/s. Similarly, an OTM-5.12 would indicate an channels that span five wavelengths and can operate at either 2.5 or 10 Gbits/s.

When OTMs are sent on the network, they are sent as 64-byte (512-bit) frames. There are four regions to the frame. The frame alignment area is used for network operational purposes. Then there are three overhead areas—optical channel transport unit (OUT) specific overhead area, optical channel payload unit (OPU) specific overhead area, and the optical channel data unit (ODU) specific overhead area—all describe various facets of the optical channel (see Figure 8.13).

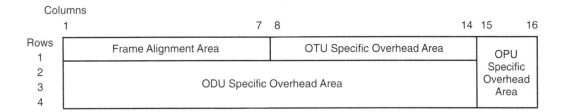

Figure 8.13
Structure of an OTM frame.

SHORT CUTS...

New devices are emerging that combine core SONET functionalities into a single box. Others go a step further and add an assortment of other functions including ATM, frame, and IP switching.

Metro DWDM gear advocate assigning different services to different wavelengths. While this approach offers capacity and flexibility, a low-enough price tag remains a challenge.

DTM is a SONET-like protocol that is especially suited to delivering real-time video streams.

10 Gbits/s Ethernet extends the Ethernet protocol to the metro core. There are flavors to 10GigE—10GBase-R for single-wavelength LAN connections, 10GBase-W for WAN connection, and 10GBase-X for multiwavelength systems.

RPR is an emerging protocol from the IEEE 802.17 working group that attempts to offer SONET-like QoS and reliability with the cost and efficiency of Ethernet.

9 Going the Last Mile

In this chapter...

THE PHOTONIC KILLER

HAVING CROSSED 10,000 MILES, LIGHT FACES
ITS TOUGHEST BATTLE—THE LAST MILE.

Today, we are remarkably successful at carrying data across the country—indeed, across the world. Through the improvements in fiber manufacturing and amplification techniques, distances are surmountable. At the same time, the constant improvements in DWDM techniques mean that transcontinental or transoceanic fibers offer near-infinite capacity.

The real challenge today remains in the last mile—the distance from your home or office to the public network. It's in finding solutions that are economical, yet powerful and flexible enough to move data from one room in a city to your living room.

Unfortunately, no one technology today meets that goal entirely. All of them miss some essential ingredient. High-speed copper technologies ostensibly can use the installed copper wiring plant for faster deployment, but often the installed wiring isn't suited to high-speed transmissions, and even where it is, performance tops out at about 2 Mbits/s or so per subscriber on a good day. Where copper isn't available, providers often use broadband wireless, which can reach very-high-speed data rates, but often only at the expense of range and being affected by weather conditions.

Enter the optical technologies for the local loop—passive optical networks (PON) and, to a lesser extent, free-space optics. They enable a huge increase in performance with their own catches. PONs, of course, require a fiber plant to be installed. Few consumers today have fiber to their home. The score is a bit better with businesses, however, of which 75 percent are estimated to be within a mile of a fiber drop. Free-space optics can reach up to 10 Gbits/s speeds through the air, but are primarily limited to point-to-point connections and suffer from severe distance limitations and susceptibility to weather conditions.

THE CHALLENGE ....

The dynamics facing local networks are very different from those facing metro core or long-haul networks. While in the core of the network, capacity might be the order of the day, out at the periphery other factors, like price, play a major role.

Think about it. The base of users over which carriers can amortize a line between California and New York makes equipment costs insignificant (OK, less significant). If DWDM gear runs $1 million a pop and there are several million customers who use that equipment each month, well, the math becomes pretty simple. And if that gear can save on pulling a new fiber, a project that can easily run $100 million, then the equipment costs really become negligible. All that matters is increasing the amount of capacity one can squeeze out of each fiber.

However, the story changes with city or metropolitan area networks. As carriers extend their networks closer to home, more equipment is needed for servicing the same number of customers. The equipment's unit cost then becomes increasing important as the number of customers over which these expenditures can be itemized decreases dramatically. Instead of serving millions of customers, we're talking dozens of customers.

Bandwidth of Any Color

But it's not only equipment costs that vary between the different networks. Bandwidth granularity, the interfaces on the equipment offered, and the distances covered by the network also change (see Table 9.1).

By connecting millions of users across a region, backbone networks deal in very coarse chunks of capacity. With the kinds of traffic levels being predicted by carriers, they typically look for minimum capacity on runs about 160 wavelengths reaching up to 320 wavelengths. As traffic approaches the edges of the network, however, these requirements begin to drop dramatically. With fewer users, metro core networks run on about 32 to 64 wavelengths while carriers look for 16 wavelengths in metro access networks.

Table 9.1   Difference in Equipment Requirements

	Metro Access	Metro Core	Long Haul
Interface Granularity	155–622 Mbits/s	2.5–10 Gbits/s	10–40 Gbits/s
Distances	10–50 km	50–100 km	600–3000 km
Capacity (in lambdas)	16	32–64	160–320

Similarly, the interfaces into these networks are also very different, in terms of both capacity and the types of service provided. Long-haul nets deal with very large traffic flows ranging from 10 Gbits/s to 40 Gbits/s. This fact is often well suited to DWDM where wavelengths start at 2.5 Gbits/s.

As traffic approaches the edges of the network, however, these requirements begin to drop dramatically. With fewer users, the amount of capacity supporting traffic in the metro core networks drops to 2.5 to 10 Gbits/s and to under 2.5 Gbits/s for access networks.

Consumers in single-family dwellings just can't take advantage of the capacity of a single wavelength. Take, for example, the family of four in the not-so-distant future. Under heavy conditions, what kind of network usage might they require? Well, let's suppose this particular family is really good at multitasking with a lot of state-of-the-art gear. Then you might get two people watching two different high-definition video sessions, three people talking on the phone, one playing an online game with, for example, a 20 Mbits/s background transfer, and another doing some Web browsing. Even under those kinds of extreme cases customer bandwidth wouldn't top 60 Mbits/s and would likely be lower. By contrast, a wavelength of today's capacity nominally delivers 2.5 Gbits/s of capacity, more than 40 times the capacity required by this customer (see Table 9.2).

Corporations are a bit trickier. With the emergence of new applications, like storage networking, companies can outsource key IT functions, increasing the amount of capacity they require for their networks. Requirements here obviously are higher, though probably around an OC-3c tops. The upshot is that carriers need access net-

Table 9.2   Future Bandwidth Requirements

Type of Session	Bandwidth Requirements (in Mbits/s)	Number of Simultaneous Sessions
High-Definition Video	20	2
Web Surfing	5	1
Online Gaming	2	1
Phone Conversations	.064	3
Background File Transfer	10	1
Total	58.192	

work with a wide range of granularity. Ideally, they need equipment that can divvy a wavelength up into 64 Kbit/s chunks—STS-1 in SONET speak.

The types of interfaces and services are also very different in the local access. Customers need to be able to connect to a network with Ethernet for their typical data requirements and to a T1 or T3 for their voice requirements. Under special circumstances they might need to handle fiber channel traffic for connecting up a storage area network (SAN) or for doing high-speed mainframe connectivity. The challenge then is to provide the appropriate equipment that accommodates all of these different traffic requirements. By the time the traffic reaches the long-haul or metro core it's just a sequence of bits.

The huge distance required for long-haul transmission makes the reach of these systems critical. A long-haul transmission typically will be able to reach 80 kilometers before amplification. Metro systems are very different. Even a major city like New York is only 301 square miles. Amplification is needed, but it's hardly crucial. As most users live within a mile of the central office, amplification within the access network is a waste of money.

THE LAST MILE OF TODAY ....

Today's residential access networks and corporate access networks hold the key to the networks of tomorrow. Until high-speed local access is in place, customers can't generate the traffic demands from new entertainment and business services that will continue to drive public network growth. The challenges differ for corporate and residential access.

Start with corporations. Commercial buildings today face two major access problems. The vast majority, around 75 percent, lack any kind of fiber access. What's more, those that have fiber access are typically served off a SONET backbone.

By now we're familiar with the evils of traditional SONET from Chapters 6 and 7. It's great for voice, but SONET's rigid hierarchical architecture makes it ill suited for handling the changing nature of corporate data traffic. Carriers end up having to waste traffic on their backbones carrying frames of less than the minimal STS-1 frames.

Today's businesses are wired up in a multitude of different ways (see Figure 9.1). Very large buildings or campuses may have a SONET ADM situated in their basements with their voice PBX routers and ATM switches connected to ports on the ADM. With smaller installations, the ADMs will be located at the central offices

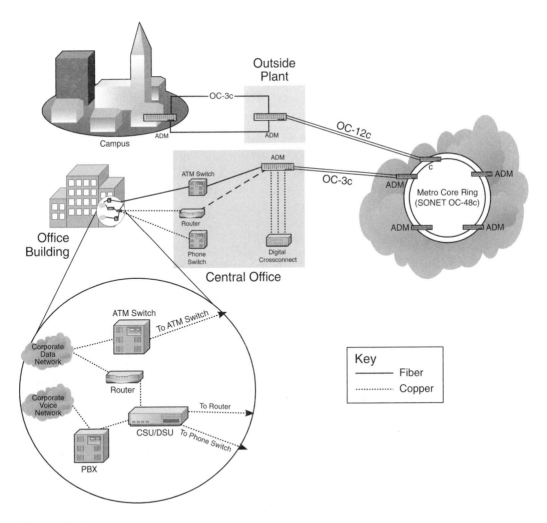

Figure 9.1
The commercial last mile.

where they'll connect to a digital crossconnect (DCS). The DCS will have one set of ports going off to a phone switch and from there to an outside plant, which will ultimately terminate as a digital connection, like a T1 line in a CSU/DSU or multiplexer, at the office building. At the same time, another set of DCS ports will go from the DCS to a router and ATM switch to an outside plant connecting to the building's networking infrastructure. At that point, another multiplexer or CSU/DSU will terminate the connection.

Residential networks are very different. Homes are connected to the phone network via copper lines that terminate at an ADM. Access to the cable TV network is via a coaxial cable drop to the home. Television signals travel across the coaxial plant to a head end where they are extracted and the appropriate content is returned.

Both of those markets are evolving. RBOCs and CLECs are delivering high-speed data access predominantly through digital subscriber line (DSL). Top speeds on DSL are difficult to predict because there are so many different types, and even then performance depends on line conditions. With that said, asynchronous DSL (ADSL), the most widely deployed DSL technology, can reach theoretical 8.192 Mbits/s to a subscriber, and 768 Kbits/s up to the network provider. Realistically, performance usually tops out much lower than that.

Compared to optic speeds, those numbers might sound pitiful, but remember: ADSL doesn't require new wiring, and that's key. New equipment is another matter. At the customer premise, an ADSL modem typically takes an Ethernet signal from a computer, converts the signal to ATM cells or HDLC frames, and puts it over an upstream channel on the ADSL line. At the carrier's end, a DSLAM or DSL access multiplexer (DSLAM) takes the DSL signals off the line and puts them out on the data or voice network. The DSLAM also takes incoming signals and sends them down to the customer via the faster downstream channel (see Figure 9.2).

Higher-speeds are available through the emerging VDSL (very high rate digital subscriber line) specification. At the time of this writing, the maximum downstream rate under consideration for VDSL is up to 52 Mbits/s with symmetrical speeds of 26 Mbits/s over lines up to 1000 ft (300 meters) in length.

The big problem, though, with both DSL implementations is getting them to work at their touted speeds. Real-world line conditions, like bridged taps and extension lines, affect DSL speeds. The is rate adaptive, so the performance of DSL decreases as distance from the DSLAM increases (see Figure 9.3).

What's more, VDSL brings its own share of problems. Interference, for example, is a problem. If strewn above ground, the VDSL lines could act as an antenna, radiating and receiving energy into amateur radio bands. Preventing this interference could further limit distances.

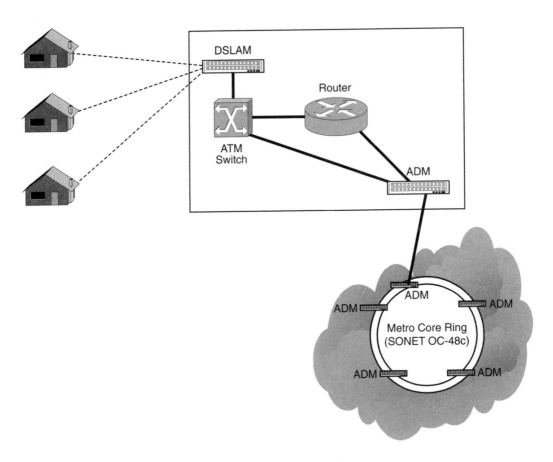

Figure 9.2
DSL-equipped homes.

The second problem is going to be the design of the customer premises gear. System management, reliability, regulatory constraints, and migration concerns favor a scheme like ADSL and ISDN, where the device is powered and can operate like a hub. Multiple devices could then plug into that hub to gain access to the VDSL link, much like a LAN.

Cost considerations, though, favor a cheaper, passive network interface with a VDSL interface installed in the customer's equipment and upstream multiplexing handled much like a LAN. Cost is particularly important here, as the VDSL gear sitting the curb services only a few users, over which the common equipment costs, like fiber links, interfaces, and equipment cabinets, must be amortized. VDSL therefore must have a much lower cost target than ADSL, whose DSLAM can sit in the CO and service far more customers.

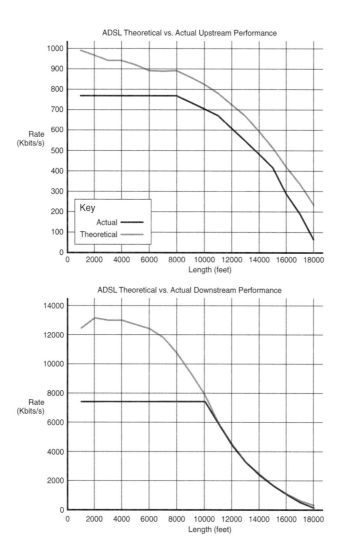

Figure 9.3
Upstream and downstream ADSL performance (Source: Orckit Communications, Ltd., Tel Aviv, Israel).

Hybrid Fiber-Coax (HFC)

At about the time that the phone companies began to reassess their infrastructure, cable TV companies underwent a similar change. Although cable TV was designed for one-way, analog transmission, the underlying coaxial cable infrastructure has the capacity for bidirectional, fast Internet access using 10 Mbits/s Ethernet.

The challenge, however, was to develop an architecture where a relatively small number of consumers would share Ethernet's capacity. The nature of standard Ethernet signaling is such that, as a significant number of users start to use the network, individual performance decreases dramatically. Existing cable TV plants, often connect 50,000 to 60,000 homes, far too many for high-speed Internet access over a common Ethernet network. What's more, offering Internet access over copper could have led to noise funneling, where every device connected to the return path on the cable network could contribute noise sufficient to block transmission signals.

By replacing part of the coaxial cable with fiber optics and using the individual cable drops at each end, these problems were solved without having to pull fiber to each home. These new plants situate fiber nodes every 500 to 2000 homes, with coaxial cable stemming from the nodes to the homes. Each node functions as an Ethernet switch, turning each cluster of homes into an Ethernet network (see Figure 9.4).

With this setup, each fiber node is allocated a 6 MHz upstream path. Cable modems equipped with Ethernet addresses are installed at the respective homes. The modems take Ethernet data in on one end, modulate the signal onto a carrier frequency, and then send the data out as on this 6-MHz signal in the 5–40 MHz range on the cable network. Access to the network is regulated, as with any Ethernet network. The data travels along the upstream path to the **headend**, where the signal is demodulated and put out onto the Internet.

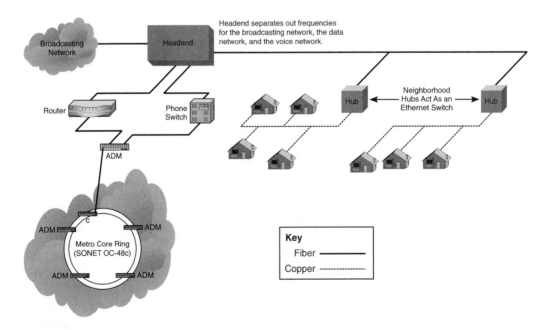

Figure 9.4
The cable modem network.

The process is similar when the headend sends data. The network traffic is sent downstream on a shared, 150-KHz Ethernet channel ranging from 54 to 350 MHz or 54 to 750 MHz. All of the homes see the respective traffic, only extracting data with their individual Ethernet address. The result is that typically cable modems deliver upstream performance of about 300 Kbits/s and downstream performance of 1–1.5 Mbits/s.

While effective today, cable modem technology faces two challenges. Businesses, where the demand exists for truly high-speed access, are still largely unserved by cable TV plants. What's more, cable modem performance is erratic, depending on the number of users utilizing the network. Adding more customers lowers the bandwidth available to each customer.

Broadband Wireless

What are carriers to do if there is no existing fiber infrastructure and if the copper infrastructure is inadequate for DSL? Enter the fixed wireless technologies—spread spectrum, LMDS, and MMDS all provide ways to deliver better than modem speeds sans the wires. Like wired architecture, these wireless network architectures come either as point-to-point connection, where the bandwidth is shared between two devices, or point-to-multipoint, where the bandwidth is shared among all of the subscribers on the network. The differences lie in their operating frequencies and, by extension, their throughput and range.

Like optical networks, wireless nets work along certain frequency ranges. Of course, where optical networks use the capacity of a fiber, wireless networks use the capacity of the radio spectrum. This spectrum gets divided and subdivided into bands as defined by the frequencies. Some bands are unlicensed, while others require a special license to operate in them.

Spread-spectrum networks operate in the unlicensed band of around 2.5 Ghz. Many of these products were adapted from wireless LANs based on the IEEE 802.11 standard that operated at the same frequency. Although in theory these devices can reach 11 Mbits/s, in reality performance is far less, topping out at around 6 Mbits/s with a cell radius of up to 8 km. This capacity is then shared among users for individual performance of around 256 Kbits/s.

The multipoint multichannel distribution system (**MMDS**) has better performance mainly because it uses a licensed band at 2.1 to 2.7 Ghz. License holders have exclusive use of 72 MHz, or 36 Mbits/sec of theoretical bandwidth, per cell across a 45-km cell radius. However, the capacity is shared among all the users in the cell. Early implementations tout a maximum performance of 5 Mbits/sec downstream and 256 Kbits/sec upstream (though 512 Kbits/sec to 1 Mbit/sec is more typical of downstream performance) for $40 to $50 per month for a consumer package, or $100 to $200 for a business package.

Current implementations of MMDS require line of sight; the antenna on the user's home needs to be able to "see" the central bay station, limiting its use in certain areas, such as those that are heavily forested. Enhancements to MMDS are enabling what's called near-line-of-sight, where smaller antennas are used and placed through out the region, enabling the equipment to "peer around" walls to reach the antennas.

However, optical speeds can be reached only with techniques running at higher frequencies. Local multipoint distribution system (**LMDS**) is also a licensed technology running at 27.5 and 31.5 GHz. The spectrum there was fairly empty, enabling the FCC to allocate larger channels within a region for a total of 1300 MHz within a region. CLECs across 493 regions received 1150 MHz in each region, permitting sufficient spectrum to offer high-speed alternatives to incumbents and cable operators. Top speeds run at 155 Mbits/s but are limited to just eight per kilometer cell. Line of sight is still required.

LAST MILE OF TOMORROW ....

Over the near term DSL, cable modems, and broadband wireless offer viable interim paths for broadband data. As traffic requirements increase, new technologies are required. Even with technology like VDSL, which can offer very high data rates over existing copper, a solution must be found for bringing the equipment as close to the customer as economically possible to maximize performance.

Optical vendors are settling on three ways to deliver this new last mile. Some vendors are using the WDM technologies of metro core out at the access network (see Chapter 7). More prominent, however, are **passive optical networks (PONs)** that lower costs by eliminating active, or powered, components. Proprietary WDM schemes extend fiber to the customer premises and then carry different traffic over different wavelengths. Free-space optics (FSO) tries to deliver optical-like performance as a wireless network.

PONs

Back in 1995 a group of telecommunications providers joined together to create a single global specification for delivering high-speed access in the last mile. Today, the group, called the Full Service Access Network (FSAN), has 21 telecommunications operators and numerous equipment suppliers, but the objective remains the same: To develop an inexpensive access technology that can be serve any type of service (hence the name "Full Service").

The result is the PON specification. By eliminating regenerators and active equipment used to bring fiber from the central office to between the customer premises, PONs reduce fiber's deployment and installation costs.

FSAN wasn't the first to push PONs. The ideas of a PON had been talked about for at least a decade prior to FSAN, but the developments in optics enabled high-speed PONs to become a reality. The specification was later proposed to the ITU, the standards body governing the formation of international telecommunication regulation, and later became known as the g.983 family of standards within the ITU.

A VIEW FROM THE FIELD: THE CASE FOR PONS

Passive optical networks (PONs) have long been understood to be the lowest-cost optical network architecture to connect a telephone central office with business or residential customers. Yet exactly what is the business case for PONS?

Recently, SBC did a study comparing the cost of a PON fiber infrastructure to both dedicated single fiber and dedicated copper infrastructures. The cost study examined the outside plant cost (materials and labor) for a new, residential subdivision and did not include the cost of network electronics. Key results from the study show that a point-to-point fiber network will typically be more expensive than a PON network, even for very short distances from the central office; labor costs play an important role here. For example, a dedicated-fiber single-fiber network can require up to 32 times the number of splices needed in a PON network. The study also found fiber PON network prove-ins vs. copper networks similar to those of digital loop carrier; close to the central office copper networks are less expensive to deploy, but about 2 miles from the CO PON solutions prove-in.

So, why aren't PONs deployed everywhere in the network today? There are two main issues. First, the cost of the PON electronics has been too high to justify deployment, even if the cost of the PON fiber network were zero. Driving down the cost of PON equipment was the key motivation for the FSAN initiative. SBC and other network operators from around the world realized that if a common PON specification met their collective needs, suppliers would have an incentive to invest in PON components and systems, since there would be a worldwide market. Recently, ITU standards based on contributions from participating FSAN companies have been adopted, and compliant PON products are available in the market. In the case of fiber-to-the-home, the cost of electronics at the customer's home will need to be less than $500; we believe such prices will be achieved in standardized products soon.

The second key problem is the cost of deploying the PON fiber network itself. Although FSAN-based PONs were originally designed for Fiber-To-The-Home (FTTH) applications, SBC has started deploying PONs for delivery of services to small businesses. Here, the business customer's need for bandwidth and willingness to pay for bandwidth is greater. This greater revenue can justify a higher PON equipment price and also justify the cost of placing fiber to some small business customers. It is an unfortunate fact of life that the cost of trenching down the street to install optical fiber does not follow Moore's law but instead is relatively fixed. For this reason FTTH deployments make the most sense in new residential developments where fiber can be placed before the streets are paved for the first time.

—By Ralph Ballart[*]

[*] Ralph Ballart is the vice president of Broadband Infrastructure and Services, SBC Technology Resources, the group responsible for broadband network element requirements and testing for SBC.

A PON, or an **optical access network (OAN)** as its formally called, is a treelike structure consisting of several branches, called **optical distribution networks (ODNs).** The ODNs run from the central office out to the customer premises using a mix of passive branching components, passive optical attenuators and splices (see Figure 9.5).

Three types of active devices can be used in a PON. At the central office, carriers install a special kind of switch, called an optical line terminal (OLT). The OLT either generates light signals on its own or takes in SONET signals (such as OC-12) from a collocated SONET crossconnect and broadcasts this traffic through one or more outgoing subscriber ports. This optical signal is received by either an optical network unit (ONU) or an optical network termination (ONT) and converted into an electrical signal for use in the customer premises.

The choice between an ONT and ONU depends on how closely the fiber extends to the home or business. When fiber extends to the home or to the building—appropriately called **Fiber to the Home (FTTH)** or **Fiber to the Building/Curb (FTTB/C)**, respectively—an ONT is located in the customer premises. If fiber does not extend to the building, as is often the case with residential customers, then an ONU is located at the curb in the case of **Fiber To The Curb (FTTC)** or even further away in a telecommunications cabinet located at the street, **Fiber To The Cabinet (FTTCab)**. DSL is then used with both FTTC and FTTCab to bring the signal to the customer premises. These four scenarios are generically called **FTTx** (see Figure 9.6).

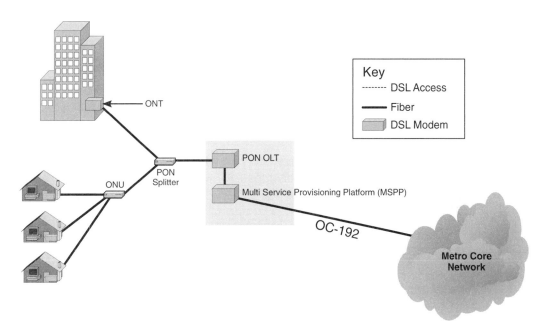

Figure 9.5
The PON network.

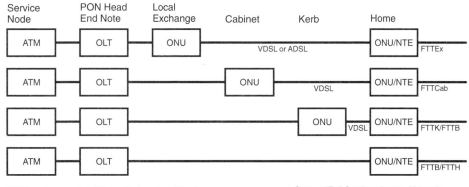

ADSL = Asymmetric Digital Subscriber Line/Loop
FTTB = Fiber to the Building
FTTCab = Fiber to the Cabinet
FTTEx = Fiber to the Exchange
FTTH = Fiber to the Home
FTTK = Fiber to the Kerb
NTE = Network Termination Equipment

Source: "Full Services Access Network
Requirements Specification"

OLT = Optical Line Termination
ONU = Optical Network Unit
PON = Passive Optical Network
VDSL = Very High Speed Digital Subscriber Line Loop

Figure 9.6
The Fiber To The "x" (FTTx) family.

PON WORKINGS ....

Across their treelike form, PONs use a combination of wave-division multiplexing (WDM), time-division multiplexing (TDM), and an access protocol, either ATM or increasing gigabit Ethernet (see Figure 9.7).

ATM PONs, or **APONs** as they're called, work as big ATM networks. Customers establish virtual circuits (VCs) across the PON to the destination, such as another office or the ISP's premises. These circuits are bundled into what's known as virtual paths (VPaths) for faster switching in the carrier's network.

APONs deliver two types of operation—symmetrical and asymmetrical. APONs can operate in all instances symmetrically, where transmission to and from the OLT occurs at the same rate, OC-3 speeds (155.52 Mbits/s). Asymmetrical performance is also defined for all the scenarios except for FTTH. With asymmetrical APONs, the downstream transmission—that is, the transmission from the OLT in the central office to the ONU or ONT—occurs at 155.52 or 622.08 Mbits/s, and upstream transmission, from the ONU or ONT to the OLT, occurs at 155.52 Mbits/s.

Those upstream and downstream transmissions occur over two channels, which might be different wavelengths on the same cable or just two different cables. The original specification called for downstream transmission on a single fiber to occur between 1480 and 1580 nm and on dual fibers between 1260 and 1360 nanometers. Upstream transmissions always occur between 1260 and 1360 nm.

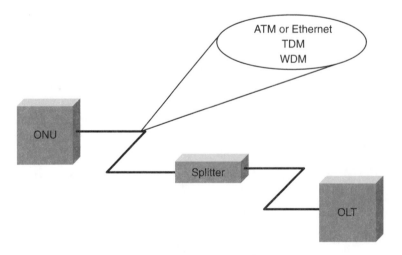

Figure 9.7
Three layers of a PON network.

A new standard adds WWDM capabilities to the APONs. With the new spec, downstream transmission is split in two, regular transmissions at 1480–1500 nm and a new enhanced band at 1539 and 1565 nm.

This new band has been defined for future applications, like broadcast video service or private circuit services for an individual ONT. Depending on the density of the channels, which impacts the quality and cost of the laser used, APONs can now support 16 wavelengths (with 200-GHz spacing between channels) or 32 wavelengths (with 100-GHz spacing between channels). However, keep in mind that since customers need one wavelength for transmission and the other for receiving, these numbers are in effect cut in half.

If there's bad news at all, it's that to implement these new channels, equipment will likely become more expensive. Since the new spectrum is narrower, there can be less drift in the laser. This means that PON equipment delivering WWDM will likely need to implement a DFB quality laser and not the cheaper Fabry-Perot lasers.

Across the main band from 1480 to 1500 nm, APONs run a TDM architectures across the send and receive channels. Within these time slots the network behaves like a LAN implementing Ethernet or ATM.

Access to the network is relegated by the OLT using a complex frame structure. Both the upstream and downstream channels are divided into frames and time slots. The exact size of each depends on the configuration. Within a symmetrical network, for example, downstream frames consist of 56 time slots—54 for data and 2 for management information. Each time slot is in turn equal to an ATM cell, 53 bytes (see Figure 9.8). Upstream frames are 53 times slots long, but run 56 bytes each. The additional three bytes are overhead that can be programmed for a variety of purposes by the OLT such as requesting an ONU to transmit a PLOAM cell or a minislot for gathering various types of management information. Asymmetrical APONs use frame-time slots configurations that are four times greater on the downstream to accommodate the 622 Mbits/s speeds.

There are two types of cells used in the APON specification. Data cells carry a variety of information including user data, signaling information, and operations and management (OAM) information. **PLOAM (Physical Layer Operations and Maintenance)** cells pass information about the physical infrastructure around the network. Carried in PLOAMs are grants, those codes supplied by the OLT allowing access to the network. OLTs can also divide up the timeslot into minislots to gather information about the ONU's traffic queues to implement QoS or Dynamic Bandwidth Allocation (DBA) as it's called by the standard.

Here's how they all work. Once an APON is operational, then a carrier can add an ONT while the system is active. Periodically, the OLT makes a gap in the upstream time slot of a few hundred microseconds and sends a special permission, a ranging grant, which can be answered by anyone. New devices seeing the ranging grant re-

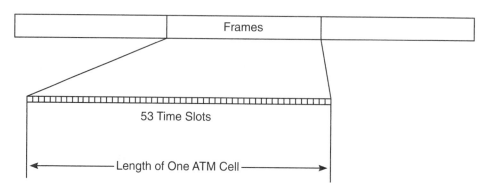

Figure 9.8
Anatomy of a PON frame.

spond with their unique serial number. When the OLT receives the acknowledgement, it configures the ONT with the information needed to join the APON. This information means an APON ID and two kinds of **grant numbers**—a PLOAM grant number and a Data grant numbers. These will be used to access the network

Then ATM kicks in. When the OLT sends an ATM cell down the APON, every ONT compares the cell's Vpath identifier against its own. If there's a match, the ONT copies the cell and removes it from the network and sends it to the customer premises. Each premises compares the cell's virtual circuit identifier against its own. If there's a match, then the node copies the data and removes the cell.

When an ONT needs to send information, it waits for a PLOAM cell to be sent by the OLT. Each PLOAM cells has 26 or 27 grants that can be read by anyone. The ONT checks the data grant number in the PLAOM cell. When it sees its grant number, it uses the grants to send the data. Then the cell gets transmitted upstream. The OLT receiver receives the bits, using the preamble to recover the clock, reads out the cells, and then passes them up to the ATM switch.

Security and QoS

Both security and QoS have been hot areas in APONs. Security on the APON is tricky, because based on our discussion so far, any ONT could read cells. There's no inherent security mechanism to prevent intrusion. The idea here is that any access network, even the voice network, can be tapped easily enough. If someone wants security, then they need to employ encryption or pay for an encrypted service where the provider adds encryption devices to the network.

With that said, the current APON specification does provide some rudimentary form of security, called scrambling. Here each cell's payload is run through an encryption algorithm that changes data using a very short encryption key of 24 bits, hence the term **scrambled**. Even 40-bit keys are considered weak. Security is improved somewhat by changing the encryption key on the fly.

While ATM provides for different types of circuits, the current APON specification does not. Every traffic flow is treated equally. A new ITU standard will add **dynamic bandwidth allocation (DBA)** to APON. DBA allows the OLT to determine who has the data to send and then sends more grants in response to that information. OLT does this by sending a mini slot grant. The ONT replies with the information about its queues, indicating the number of cells to be transmitted. The OLT then measures the amount of data to be sent against the type of service purchased by that customer, the existing traffic conditions, and the like. Based on that information, the OLT then issues a grant and the ONT responds in the normal manner.

Management and Survivability

Public networks aim to be nothing if not reliable. Forget the increased performance, enhanced security, and improved QoS that APONs can offer. Without adequate uptime, no service will be in business very long, and that means providing adequate management and fault tolerance.

The management part is supplied through the POAM cells. Those allow ONTs to report back to the OLT about themselves. The same cells are also used to provide certain bit patterns that can be used to align lasers and measure power output.

On the fault-tolerance side, an emerging APON specification will provide for redundancy in the network. Under this scenario the APON works like SONET's dual-ring configuration. Each ONT connects to two OLTs. Two protection scenarios are then possible. One-to-one protection lets the transmitter choose which line to use and leaves the other untouched. This configuration then could be used by providers to put UBR traffic on the backup line, with the understanding that in the event of a failure the traffic will be bumped from the network.

The second approach is called 1+1 protection. Under this scenario, transmitters and receivers on both sides of the network pick the cleaner line to communicate over. This way, in the event of a switchover no traffic is lost from the backup line (see Figure 9.9).

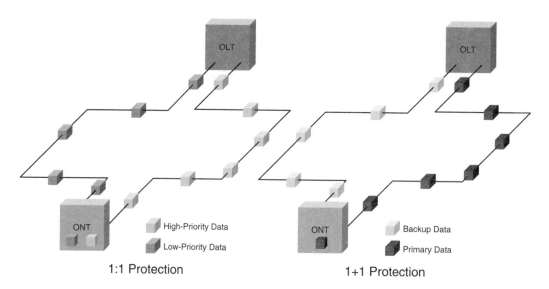

1:1 Protection   1+1 Protection

Figure 9.9
With 1:1 protection, the backup line is used to carry lower-priority data. This is lost when the primary line fails over. Higher resilience is provided with 1+1 protection, where the same data is sent over both lines and the ONU and OLT constantly select the better of the two data sets.

EPONS AND ETHERNET IN THE FIRST MILE............

A three-time champion is warming up for the PON ring. Having defeated token ring, then FDDI, and then ATM in the corporate networks, Ethernet is getting set to stretch its tentacles into the public network through the creation of **EPONs** or Ethernet passive optical networks.

Today the PON specifications call for the use of ATM cells, but ATM is far from ideal. As we discussed in Chapter 2, ATM is adept at delivering voice and data. It offers the ability to insure quality of service, which is what you need to support voice and video. And it works with much of the existing telecom infrastructure.

These are all good things. The problem with ATM is twofold. On the technical side, there's the nasty cell-tax issue, which means that ATM wastes bandwidth when it starts carrying IP traffic. This is because ATM cells are very short (53 bytes), so capacity ends up being wasted on overhead traffic and inter-frame spacing.

Then there's also the Ethernet issue. Corporate networks and home networks aren't based on ATM. They use ATM. So network operators—and for that matter, customers—end up paying, even if only indirectly, for equipment that has to convert from ATM to Ethernet and back to ATM.

Does that sound kind of dumb? It does to lots of networking folk, which is why they've begun to develop EPONs. Moving Ethernet over the last mile isn't as simple as it sounds. Although the protocol is immensely popular, some significant enhancements need to occur before it can take on the last mile.

Carriers need networks that won't fail. Ever. Today, this means two things. To prevent and troubleshoot failures there needs to be a way of gathering low-level statistics about the network's operation. At the same time, there needs to be a recovery mechanism for quickly avoiding failures in the network. Neither of those are provided within the traditional Ethernet specification.

To address those challenges, and others, the IEEE working group responsible for Ethernet, 802.3, formed the Ethernet in the First Mile (EFM) study group to address the challenge of forming an EPON. Work is just beginning at press time with the group having drafted a project authorization request (PAR). The next step will be to become full task force (expected to be called 802.3ah), which is able to formally begin work on a standard.

As such, the EPON details are still pretty much an unknown. What is known is that the standard will reuse existing Ethernet standards insofar as possible. This means that the media access control (MAC) layer, or how Ethernet shares access to the line, will remain unchanged. However, as the standards will likely be full duplex, the basic CSMA/CD protocol will be unused. Instead, upstream and downstream transmission will occur on two different channels. The basic performance of the network will also be based on previous standards. Currently two speeds are being investigated—1 Gbit/s and 10 Mbits/s.

What will be different, however, is the architecture, the types of medium over which the Ethernet spec will run, and the operations and management information supplied by the protocol. Two basic network architectures are being defined—point-to-multipoint and point-to-point. Point-to-multipoint technology enables a single device in a carrier's premise to transmit data to multiple subscribers. The group will specify point-to-multipoint for fiber only. Point-to-point networks where there's a line for every subscriber will be defined for fiber and for copper.

Four physical interfaces are being defined. On the fiber side, the group aims to standardize a 1 Gbit/s interface for PON. The spec will work for distances of up to least 10 kilometers and possibly longer. Point-to-point links are also being defined. There will be a 1 Gbit/s (100base-X) option running over single mode fiber for up to 10 kilometers. There will be at least a 10 Mbits/s option for running 2500 feet over single-pair, nonloaded voice-grade copper.

Management is the other big change to the specification. The standard will include at least three categories of management information. Remote failure indication will inform the device at the carrier premises whether a device has failed. Remote loopbacks enable the carrier to test the transmission side as seen from the CPE, and link monitoring will enable carriers to monitor the network for errors and failures. Additional measures, such as fault isolation and provisions for accounting and billing, are also being considered.

Evaluating Ethernet individually is always misleading, and that's certainly the case with EFM. Criteria for quality of service, for guaranteeing the low-level performance characteristic, and network security for insuring privacy will likely not be included in the EFM specification.

Yet, that doesn't mean there's no provision for these standards. Both will likely be covered in complementary specifications in other IEEE working groups. The all-important QoS will likely be handled though 802.1q and security through 802.10 as discussed in Chapter 2.

WIRELESS OPTICS ....

Even in ideal circumstances, though, these optical schemes won't hit the majority of the market for some time. If carriers upgrade only 5 percent of their installed cabling each year, then it could be another 10 years before most customers start to see fiber installations.

While DSL, cable, and broadband wireless technologies will service the majority of suppliers then, some providers are touting an alternative scheme, free-space optics. These systems propogate optical signals through air by sending signal in the terahertz frequencies.

By using optical transceivers, **free-space optics (FSO)** can deliver speeds of 155 Mbits/s to 10 Gbits/s. By eliminating the fiber, FSO vendors claim to dramatically cut installation costs. One vendor has estimated that it can reduce the cost of running fiber to a building from around $100,000 to $200,000 per building to $20,000 per building.

The bad news? FSO are point-to-point devices. Thus, while they may be appropriate for delivering very fat pipes to individual building, their utility in providing a generalized local access solution is nominal.

Even distance limitations are going to factor. FSO links can reach up to one or two kilometers, but that's on a good day. Environmental conditions limit their range and reliablity (see Table 9.3). To reach 99.99 to 99.999 percent uptime per year—or to put that another way, 5 to 53 minutes of downtime per year—the FSO link needs to be within 200 meters. Fiber-based solutions, of course, have far greater reach, ranging between 30 and 40 kilometers.

Table 9.3   Loss Rates for FSO Networks

Atmospheric Conditions	Sample Loss
Clear	−5 to −15 dB/km
Rain	−20 to −50 dB/km
Snow	−20 to −150 dB/km
Fog	−50 to −350 dB/km

Source: "Wireless Optical Networking," Scott Bloom, Air Fiber, Supercomm 2001.

SHORT CUTS..

The dynamics of the access network are very different from those of the core and the metro core. Cost, granularity of bandwidth, and range of interfaces are all critical.

Most corporate customers have two problems with their network. On the one hand they lack fiber, and on the other hand they're often forced to purchase more capacity than is required.

Residential customers who want fast Internet access can choose between DSL, cable modem technology, or broadband wirelsss. All are limited in either their performance, range, or predicatability.

The main optical solutions for the local access, then, are passive optical networks (PONs) and free-space optics. Many providers have proprietary WDM implementations as well.

PONs reduce costs by eliminating active equipment from the infrastructure. Today APONs are prominent, with EPONs coming in fast.

Free-space optics deliver optical speeds on point-to-point links, but are very limited by the environmental conditions.

10 Optical Signaling

In this chapter...

SONET ASPIRES FOR GREATNESS.

A network is not the sum of its parts. With all of the switches and multiplexers, 10 Gigabits/s Ethernet or enhanced SONET, you won't have an intelligent network. What's missing is some way to closely knit the optical layer with the application.

That's where signaling and next-generation routing come into play. Both the packet and circuit worlds are developing new architectures and standards to enable carriers to deploy faster, more responsive, multivendor optical networks.

These changes are happening at a number of different levels, many of which have little to do with underlying transmission of optical signals per se. Routing protocols are being overhauled to enable networks to grow or scale to more devices. New interfaces between devices are being defined for faster configuration. The optical layer itself is being made smarter so that devices treat DWDM links as complete paths and not discrete chunks. Finally, the technology is being developed to enable applications to control the underlying optical layers.

Each of these subjects alone could (and does) constitute entire books. We'll touch on the drivers and the outlines of these solutions, referencing the implementation details as necessary.

BRINGING THE TWO TOGETHER.........................

The final step toward building the intelligent optical network is to bind the applications with the underlying optical layer. Today, the public network is largely ignorant of the type of traffic being transported across the network. Whether it's IP or voice, a video call or an email, all of the traffic receives optimum service. Capacity is reserved in the network for an unspecified duration or if specified then for weeks or months. As carriers look at ways to cut costs, however, there's increasing interest in delivering just the right amount of the capacity with just the right attributes only for the necessary time. To reach that goal, the underlying optical network needs to be configured for each individual traffic stream.

Two basic approaches are emerging for enhancing the interaction between the data and the underlying transport. The peer-to-peer model argues for a single network, where the equipment at the edge, largely data equipment, is responsible for deciding how bandwidth gets allocated within the core of the network. The distinctions between the data and the underlying optical networks are blurred, as the peer-to-peer model sees a merging of the signaling protocols needed to establish and tear down connections.

It's an ambitious approach, given that today carriers are very skeptical of one another and preciously guard the details of their internal networks. Not surprisingly, the peer-to-peer model is largely promoted by data vendors accustomed to the rich heritage of collaboration in the Internet.

The overlay model takes a far more traditional avenue and basically calls for maintaining two discrete networks—an optical layer and a network layer. The optical layer will take requests from data equipment as well as other types of gear for establishing and tearing down circuits or paths. The view taken is fundamentally hierarchical, where the devices within a certain domain see more of the network than do those outside that domain. This calls for instituting **user network interfaces** (UNIs) to shield the complexity (and the provider's crown jewels) from those on the outside while using **network to network interfaces (NNIs)** to disclose that information to devices on the interior of the network. Traditional voice operators tend to back the overlay model.

PEER TO PEER MODEL...................................

In order to realize the peer-to-peer model, a consistent signaling scheme needs to be implemented across all infrastructure equipment. Easy, right? Hardly. Such a process is a huge undertaking. The IETF, the folks who define the underlying protocols that run the Internet, largely address the challenge today by extending multiprotocol label switching (MPLS) to cover non-IP devices. To better understand this new protocol, called generalized MPLS (GMPLS), let's look at some of the drivers behind MPLS, how the protocol operates, and then what's different about GMPLS.

Problems with Routing Today

There's a widespread belief among the data network community that IP can be adapted to carry all types of traffic—from voice to Web surfing, email to video. While an enhanced underlying network is required, the very operation of IP also needs to be altered for all sorts of reasons. The reasons include scalability, complexity, performance, upgradability, and QoS enforcement.

Scalability became a big problem in the Internet. As the number of nodes increased, more paths, or routes, for reaching those nodes were formed. These routes began to swamp the databases, called routing tables, that routers use for moving packets from one destination to another. Also the increasing number of packets that needed to be processed between locations extracted even stiffer performance penalties from the routers.

And then there was the ATM issue. The complexity and scalability of carrying IP traffic over ATM was becoming a huge problem. Routers were connected together largely through ATM virtual circuits. To maximize performance, those circuits were constructed as a full mesh; that is, each router on the ATM network was connected with every other router (see Figure 10.1).

This creates the problem that, in effect, every router is adjacent to every other router on that network, regardless of their physical location. Under existing routing protocols, adjacent routers update each other with information about the changes to the network. With a few routers in the network the amount of routing information that's generated is nominal, but as the number of routers increases, every n new routers entail n^4 new updates. Since the amount of routing information grows so quickly, large networks can reach the point where just the routing traffic can overwhelm the router. Work-arounds are possible, but typically not without some sacrifice of sacrificing on performance or simplicity.

Routing performance has another dynamic as well—competition. Layer 2 switches, like Ethernet switches, offer far better performance than their routing cousins at far less cost. Small wonder: layer 2 switches typically provide a fraction of a router's functionality. What's more, since they look only at the layer 2 address and not the layer 3 address, they can begin processing the packet sooner.

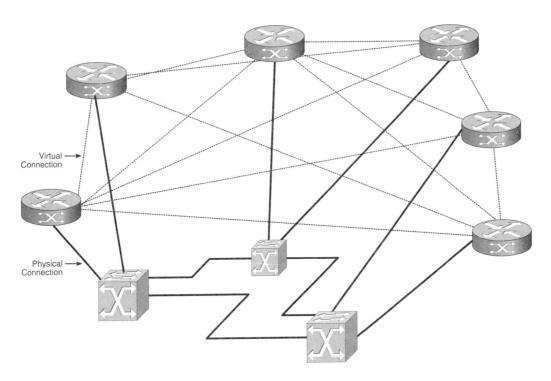

Virtual → Connection

Physical → Connection

Figure 10.1
With ATM, routers are often connected with a full mesh of virtual circuits.

Routers are still needed in the network to do the route calculations needed to effectively move packets across the country. Increasingly, though, there's been interest in trying to adapt the switching model to routing.

Upgrading to new routing functionality also became notoriously difficult. One example is deploying what's called classless interdomain routing (CIDR). To put it simply, CIDR enhances a variety of IP addressing problems, always a hot topic for IP networks. Anyway, deploying CIDR requires changing the forwarding algorithms of nearly all routers—a very time-consuming and costly process.

Finally, there's the problem of carrying varying types of traffic. Increasingly there's interest among some providers in carrying different types of traffic over an IP network. This necessarily entails quality of service (QoS), discussed in Chapter 2. However, QoS alone isn't sufficient. Currently IP schemes that attempt to address just the QoS problem fail because paths become overprovisioned with IP traffic. Routers will first converge on a particular route as having the least cost. Once selected, the QoS protocol will start to assign traffic to this path. At some point the path will run out of resources, but the routers will still favor it, causing the QoS to fail. A solution is needed that integrates QoS and routing together.

EMERGENCE OF MPLS ··

The answer to this dilemma has been to devise a new way of routing IP traffic, called multiprotocol label switching (MPLS). Unlike typical routing, MPLS works on the idea of flows. Flows are a string of packets between two common end points. Traditional routing works by looking inside routing tables for the appropriate routes for each packet. Every router populates these routing tables by running routing protocols to identify the shortest and or fastest route through the network between any two points (see Figure 10.2).

By contrast, MPLS does the route calculation once on each packet flow through a provider's networks. The route is then embedded inside each packet as a string of labels (hence the name)—short, fixed-length values typically embedded inside the link layer or referenced by the link layer. Routers along the way read these labels and use them to do faster lookups, reducing processing time and improving router scalability.

Of course, that's a gross simplification of a pretty complex process. Let's watch a path a packet may take between two points. When a packet leaves your PC, it makes its way across the network, ultimately hitting what's called a **label-edge router (LER)**, likely located at the entrance to the carrier's network. The LER is the door-

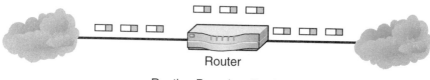

Routing Based on Packets

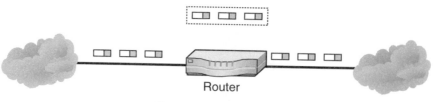

Routing Based on Flows

Figure 10.2
Traditional routing does a lookup for every packet that traverses a router. With MPLS, lookups occur once for each set of traffic flows—strings of packets between two destination points.

keeper to the MPLS network. As packets travel through the LER, they're examined and their route that they need to take is identified using typical routing protocols modified for MPLS's unique requirements. Thus there are **OSPF-TE** (for traffic engineering) and **BGP-TE**. With these protocols, network designers can assign various parameters to links and then use that information to maximize the efficiency of their networks, a process called traffic engineering.

The packets are also grouped together into traffic flows called **forward equivalence classes (FEC)**. Each FEC describes a type of traffic flow between two logical points, such as between networks, machines, or even between processes in different machines. The result is a huge number of potential FECs that can be defined.

The decision between these FECs comes down to a choice between scalability and functionality. Larger flows will scale better, since there are fewer of them. At the same time, finer flows offer more flexibility in how they get directed through the network. Carriers will typically implement a combination of the two, aggregating together, for example, company traffic flows between locations and then within them finer traffic flows reflecting specific types of service.

Once the LER determines the route and the FEC, a tag is appended to the packet. Typically, this label gets appended to the layer 2 (Ethernet, for example) header, though if room is not available within layer 2, a small reference, called a shim, is added to direct the router to the location of the label inside the data field.

To ensure that capacity for the transmission is reserved end-to-end, the LER uses a **label distribution protocol (LDP)**. The LDP, which may be RSVP or CR-LDP, enables the LER to reserve capacity along the route selected by its routing protocols and to distribute the necessary labels to direct the traffic along this route. Once completed, the label switched path (LSP) is established. Traffic sent onto to this LSP traverses the desired route specified by the LER. Each LSR reads the specific label, looks up in its table where the packets should be forwarded, and acts accordingly.

GMPLS...

With MPLS implemented, providers gain better performance and better control over their networks. At same time, though, MPLS remains limited in terms of the provisioning of bandwidth within the physical network. With the growth of DWDM and optical switching, providers have the ability to alter the amount of bandwidth on a given link. MPLS is independent of those characteristics. So if a large customer, for example an ISP, requires more bandwidth on a given link, there is no construct within MPLS to request that additional capacity.

Enter generalized Generalized MPLS (GMPLS), at one time called multiprotocol lambda switching. GMPLS extends the MPLS protocol with the necessary constructs to control not just routers but DWDM systems, ADMs, photonic crossconnects, and the like. With GMPS, providers can dynamically provision resources and provide the necessary redundancy for implementing various protection and restoration techniques.

It's important to keep in mind that, like MPLS, GMPLS is not a network layer protocol. TCP/IP networks like the Internet, for example, still require IP to function. GMPLS is a signaling protocol and is used by customer equipment to signal to other equipment to establish or tear down a circuit. That's a far cry from today's networks where capacity has to be manually "pinned" up by an network operator.

To expand beyond it's IP roots, GMPLS extends MPLS in a variety of important ways. These changes impact basic LSP proprieties, the requesting and communication of labels, the unidirectional nature of LSPs, the propagation of errors, and the information provided to synchronize initial and final LSRs of a path.

While MPLS dealt only with what GMPLS calls **packet switch capable (PSC)** interfaces, GMPLS adds four other types. **Layer-2 switch capable (L2SC)** interfaces can forward data based on content within frames and cells; **TDM capable** or just TDM interfaces forward data based on the data's time slot; **lambda switch capable (LSC)** interfaces, like a photonic crossconnect, work on individual wavelengths or wavebands, and **fiber switch cable (FSC)** interfaces work on individual or multiple fibers.

These devices establish LSPs as in MPLS. An LSP may be a routed flow of IP packets but just as easily another type of connection, like a light path or a SONET circuit. Remember that paths must start and end at common devices. An LSP that's a SONET circuit must originate and terminate at a SONET device.

These different LSPs take advantage of the nesting that occurs typically in MPLS. Within MPLS, flows are aggregated into larger flows. The same basic concept applies here, only think of the LSPs as virtual representations of physical constructs. So LSPs representing lower-order SONET circuits might be nested together within a higher-order SONET circuit. Similarly, LSPs that run between FSCs might contain those that run between LSCs, which could contain those that run between TDMs, followed by L2SC and finally PSC (see Figure 10.3).

Otherwise GMPLS functions much like MPLS. LSPs are established by using RSVP-TE or CR-LDP to send what's called a PATH/label request message. This message contains a generalized label request, often an explicit route object (ERO), and

Figure 10.3
Hierarchy of LSPs.

specific parameters for the particular technology The generalized label request is a GMPLS addition that specifies the LSP encoding type and the LSP payload type. The encoding type indicates the type of technology being considered, whether it is SONET or Gigabit Ethernet, for example. The LSP payload type identifies the kind of information being carried within that LSP's payload. The ERO more or less controls the path that an LSP takes through the network.

The message traverses a series of nodes, as in MPLS, and reaches its destination. The destination replies with the necessary labels, which are inserted into each LSR's tables along the way. Once the reply reaches the initiating LER, the LSP can be established and traffic sent to the destination.

OVERLAY MODEL ···

The fundamental problem with the peer-to-peer model is that it ignores the dynamics of today's competitive marketplace. Providers are very reluctant to disclose the internals of their networks to their competitors, and so treating them as a peer isn't always possible.

The overlay model addresses this problem by defining various interfaces into the network. Most commonly a user network interface (UNI) is specified. This is a simplified interface that hides the complexity (proprietary information) of the network from the customer. Think of it as your common telephone. You can request a circuit by picking up the phone and dialing. Other defined operations, such transferring a call, might be possible as well. However, you do all of these without knowing the underlying technology within the provider's network.

The optical internetworking forum (OIF), an industry consortium of vendors, is defining a UNI for the GMPLS specification. The UNI specifies a way for a client, called a UNI-C, to invoke transport network services with a UNI-N, a device on another provider's network. The idea here is that if a provider, say an ISP, needs more capacity in the network it signals to the carrier delivering the underlying network, who automatically activates the necessary bandwidth (see Figure 10.4).

To date, this UNI is limited to three actions. Connection creation allows a connection of specified attributes to be activated between two points. These connections may be subject to policies defined by the operator, such as user group restrictions or security procedures. Connection deletion allows an established connection to be deleted. Connection status enquiry allows nodes to retrieve certain connection parameters by querying the network. The ability to modify a connection, once established, is not currently supported.

The kinds of connections that can be established today are limited to SONET or SDH. More specifically, though, an OIF connection is a combination of the framing,

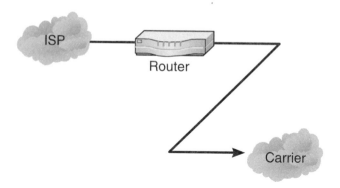

Figure 10.4
With a UNI in place, ISPs can request more capacity without knowing the carrier's underlying network.

concatenation method, transparency, and bandwidth of the signal carried. These details are summarized in Table 10.1.

Table 10.1 Connection Types

Item	Explanation
Framing	SONET or SDH
'XXX' Transparency	Clients may not modify the overhead bytes associated with the 'XXX', where 'XXX' can be section, line, or path
Signal Types	Types of SONET or SDH signals supported. Under SONET these are STS-1 SPE, STS-1, STS-3, STS-12, STS-48, STS-192, and STS-768
Concatenation	How SONET frames are combined. This can be done either as no concatenation (i.e., standard) or contiguous

ASON/ASTN...

As the IETF began working on MPLS, the ITU began developing automatic switched transport network (ASTN) and automatic switched optical network (ASON) specifications. ASTN is a superset of switched functionality applying to SONET and OTN. ASON will only apply to OTN.

Under the ITU/ANSI view the network consists of clients with varying levels or views into the network of differing functionality. The client might be a multiplexer or WDM system but could just as easily be an Ethernet client or some other client that's implementing GFP.

These clients connect into the network through one of three different types of network interfaces—user network interface (UNI), external-network-to-network interface (E-NNI), and internal-network-to-network interface (I-NNI) (see Figure 10.5). The UNI defines how a customer can access their provider's network. Only the bare-bones information is provided in this case—i.e., the name and address of the end point, authentication and admission control of the client, and connection service messages.

Carriers, however, need to provide more information among themselves and within their domains among their own network devices. E-NNIs provide reachability or summarized networked address information along with authentication and admission control and connection service messages. Think of this as an electronic address book provided by one carrier to the next of all of the available nodes. E-NNIs can also be used between two business units of the same provider or can reduce the amount of topology information exchanged between networks. With E-NNIs, the exact paths through the network aren't known to the other carrier, but the available clients that can be "called" are known. I-NNIs go one step further. This interface enables devices to

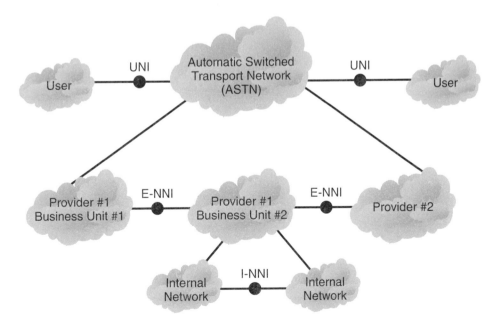

Figure 10.5
Interfaces in OTN.

get the crown jewels, the topology or routing information for the carrier's network as well as the connection service messages and information needed to optionally control network resources.

Through these interfaces clients can be connected via three different types of circuits—provisioned circuits, signaled circuits, and hybrid circuits. Provisioned circuits, also called hard-permanent circuits, are what we commonly think of as leased lines. Then, either through a network management station or manual intervention, each individual network element along a particular path is configured with the required information to establish a connection between two end points.

Signaled circuits, on the other hand, are established dynamically by the end point requesting bandwidth. These types of connections require network addressing information to establish a connection with an end point. When we dial the phone, the circuits established are signaled circuits.

The new additions here are the hybrid connections. These are a cross between provisioned and signaled circuits. Hybrid circuits have provisioned connections into the ASTN, but then rely on switched connections within the ASTN to connect with other nodes. Since they combine the two types of connection, hybrid connections are also called soft provisioned connections (SPCs). To the end node an SPC and a regular permanent circuit appear to be the same.

SHORT CUTS..

There are two basic approaches for merging the optical and data networks: the peer-to-peer model and the overlay model. The peer-to-peer model collapses the two domains together. The overlay model keeps them distinct through the use of different network interfaces.

Numerous challenges with current routing schemes led the data networking industry to develop MPLS.

With GMPLS, the IETF extends MPLS to non-IP network elements such as crossconnects or add-drop multiplexers.

GMPLS, however, presupposes equal access for all devices to network information. There is no construct of a user network interface (UNI), which was developed by the OIF.

With ASON/ASTN, client networks will be able to request services from the network.

Appendix

Key Differences between Single-Mode Fiber Specs

Key Differences Between Single-Mode Fiber Specs

Type	ITU Standard	Band	Cladding	MFD	Cutoff Wavelength	Chromatic Dispersion Coefficient	Chromatic Dispersion Slope	Min–Max Dispersion	Attenuation Coefficient	PMD Coefficient
NDSF	G.652	1310	125 ± 1 µm	8.6–9.5 µm ± 0.7	1260 nm	1300–1324 nm	0.093 ps/nm²/km	Not relevant	Up to STM-16: 1310 nm: 0.5 dB/km, 1550 nm: 0.4 dB/km; STM-16 to STM-64: 1310 nm: 0.4 dB/km, 1550 nm: 0.35 dB/km	0.5 ps/km
ZDSF	G.653	1550	125 ± 1 µm	7.8–8.5 µm ± 0.8	1270 nm	1500–1600 nm	0.085 ps/nm²/km	No minimum stated; maximum is 3.5 ps/nm/km	1550 nm: 0.35 dB/km	0.5 ps/km
NZDSF	G.655	1530–1565	125 ± 1 µm	8–11 µm ± 0.7	1480 nm	1530–1565 nm	Not stipulated	With 200 GHz channel spacing: 0.1–6 ps/nm/km; with 100 GHz channel spacing: 1–10 ps/nm/km	1550 nm: 0.35 dB	0.5 ps/km

MFD = mode field diameter
nm = nanometer
µm = micron
ps = picoseconds
km = kilometer
GHz = gigahertz
STM-16 = OC-48 = 2.5 Gbits/s
STM-64 = OC-192 = 10 Gbits/s
NDSF = non-dispersion-shifted fiber
ZDSF = zero dispersion-shifted fiber
NZDSF = nonzero dispersion-shifted fiber

Glossary

1000Base-T

The Ethernet specification for running 1000 Mbits/s over unshielded twisted pair (UTP) cabling and fiber.

100Base-T

The Ethernet specification for running 100 Mbits/s over unshielded twisted pair (UTP) cabling **and fiber**.

10Base-T

The Ethernet specification for running 10 Mbits/s over unshielded twisted pair (UTP) cabling **and fiber**.

802.1q

See VLANs.

802.3ae

The IEEE subcommittee within the 802.3 working group developing 10 Gbits/s Ethernet.

acousto-optic switches

Switches that direct light using acoustics which alter the density of different regions within a material, thereby changing the angle at which the light striking the material is deflected.

ADM

Add-drop multiplexer—a device that adds or removes select wavelengths from a line. Optical ADMs (OADM) do this on an optical line.

all-optical switches

See OOO switches.

amplifier

A device that increases the "volume" of a signal. Amplifiers are unintelligent in their operation, strengthening the signal and noise within the amplified region.

angle of incidence

The angle at which a light ray strikes an object as measured from the normal.

angle of reflection

The angle at which light bounces off an object. The angle of reflection equals the angle at which the electromagnetic wave is incident on an object as measured from the normal.

APONs (ATM PONs)
Passive optical networks that use ATM as the transport.

AS
Autonomous system—term used with routing protocols to reflect a system that's under-managed and controlled by a single entity: either a user, group, or organization. Each AS is described by an AS Number (ASN). ASN 1, for example, is registered to Genuity. Typically, BGP is used to move traffic between AS while a routing protocol like OSPF is used to route data within an AS.

ATM
Asynchronous transfer mode.

band filters
Interference filters that reflect or transmit a range of wavelengths.

Benes switch fabric
A way of extending Clos switched architecture through the use of a series of small switching elements.

BGP
Border gateway protocol—the major routing protocol used to communicate between large networks domains called autonomous systems.

BGP-TE
Border gateway protocol for traffic engineering—a routing protocol used with MPLS to calculate the shortest path between two points based on traffic engineering parameters assigned to the links by the network designer. BFP-TE is used for calculating routes between AS provider domains.

blocking
The switching instance of being unable to establish a connection between an inbound and outbound port because of an existing connection.

BLSR
Bidirectional line-switched rings—a SONET ring-protection scheme where a backup ring can be used to carry data, which is dropped in the event that the primary ring fails. A 4F-BLSR ring uses four fibers, two in each direction, and offers dedicated protection with alternative ring path and span protection. A 2F-BLSR ring uses two fibers, one in each direction, and offers dedicated protection with an alternative ring path.

BEC
Bose-Einstein condensate—the coldest material ever created, which only forms at –460° F. It is used to stop light in the labs, which ultimately may lead to developments like optical memory.

broadcast traffic
Traffic that is sent by one node to all nodes on the network.

bubble switches
Switches that direct light between ports by creating bubbles at junctures on a grid filled with a special liquid. Normally light passes through the liquid. When a bubble is formed, the light is refracted down the appropriate channel.

C-band
Conventional band—refers to the spectral range of wavelengths from 1530 to 1565 nm.

centimeter
One hundredth of a meter.

chromatic dispersion
Pulse spreading due to the different times needed for the wavelengths to propagate down the fiber.

circulator
A component that's like an isolator but connects to three or more fibers.

cladding
A thin layer of glass surrounding the fiber's core. The cladding has a lower refractive index than does the core, thus reflecting the signal back into the core.

CLECs
Competitive local exchange carriers—pronounced "see lecs," are competitive local access providers created by the Telecommunications Act of 1996.

Clos switch
A type of switch where small crossbars are used as juncture points within the switch.

coaxial
A type of cable used in early Ethernet implementations.

connectionless
A type of network where nodes can send traffic without waiting to first establish a logical connection with the destination.

connection-oriented
A type of network that must first establish a logical link between computers before data can be sent.

constructive interference
Collision of two waves that are in phase, the result being to amplify the signal.

core
The part of the fiber carrying the optical signal. The core is also used to refer to the central part of a network, the networking core.

couplers
Components that distribute optical power between ports. Passive couplers join two fibers together. Active couplers produce two separate output signals in networks.

critical angle
The point at which the angle of refraction is so great that refraction no longer occurs and light is reflected back into the original substance. This phenomenon is called total internal reflection.

crossbar switch
A type of switch where input and output ports intersect with another in a kind of matrix.

custom queuing
Procedure that gives traffic classes a predetermined amount of line capacity by assigning varying amounts of queue space to each traffic class and then servicing those queues one after another.

cut-off wavelength
The shortest wavelength at which a multimode fiber provides two or more paths for light to travel. Alternatively, the longest wavelength at which single-mode fiber carries one mode.

DBA
Dynamic bandwidth allocation—allows the OLT to determine who has data to send and then sends more grants in response to that information.

dBµ
Decibels relative to one microwatt.

DBm
Decibels relative to one milliwatt.

DBR laser
Distributed Bragg reflection laser—similar to a DFL, but has the grating placed outside the cavity.

DCS
Digital crossconnect system—device that takes incoming TDM signals and switches them between ports.

decibels
A measure of power levels.

decimeter
One tenth of a meter.

demultiplexer
A device that separates out multiplexed signals from a fiber.

destination address
The address of a station receiving a frame or packet.

destructive interference
Collision of two waves that are out of phase, the result being that they interfere with one another, degrading the signal.

detectors
Devices that detect a light pulse.

DFL
Distributed feedback laser—similar to a Fabry-Perot laser with a corrugated grating across the upper part of the cavity. This grating allows only undesired frequencies through and by extension traps light of the desired frequency in the lasing cavity.

dichroic filters
Thin films that selectively reflect or transmit various wavelengths. Dichroic filters are used in binoculars and camera lenses.

diffraction
The bending of a wave as it strikes an item shorter than its wavelength.

diffuse reflection
Reflection of parallel rays off a rough surface at different angles, causing distortion.

digital wrapper
See OTN.

direct modulation
Turning a light source on and off by changing the current passing through it.

dispersion
The spreading out of a light pulse as it travels over time.

dispersion-limiting fibers
Special fibers designed to combat chromatic dispersion.

DPT
Dynamic packet transport—Cisco's branded name for its SRP technology.

drift
The shifting of a laser's wavelength over time.

DSF
Dispersion shifted fiber—has altered characteristics to take advantage of certain lower-attenuation characteristics. See ZDSF and NZDSF.

DTM
Dynamic synchronous transfer mode—a metro core technology designed to carry video.

duplex-Ethernet
A version of the Ethernet standard that sends and receives packets on two different pairs of wires.

DWDM
Dense wavelength division multiplexing—having channel spacing of 200 GHz or less.

E-band
Extended band—referring to the spectral range of wavelengths from 1360 to 1460 nm.

EDFAs

Erbium-doped fiber amplifiers—the most widely used amplifiers today. They operate at wavelengths of 1530 to 1620 nm.

edge emitters

Lasers that emit light from the edge.

EFM

Ethernet in the first mile—an emerging standard within Ethernet that will specify the use of EPONS.

electroholographic switches

Switches that imbed holographic images of Bragg gratings within special crystals, called KLTNs (potassium lithium tantalata niobate). Normally light just passes through the crystals, but when a voltage is applied, the hologram is activated, diverting the incoming light to a specific output port.

electromagnetic radiation

Waves that are comprised of both electrical and magnetic fields moving orthogonally or perpendicular to one another.

electro-optical switches

Switches that use the electro-optic effect to change the velocity of light through a waveguide, thereby directing the light signal between ports.

encoding

The process by which bits of data are transmitted onto a fiber or wire.

EPONs (Ethernet PONs)

Passive optical networks that use Gigabit Ethernet as the transport.

ESBGs

Electrically switchable Bragg gratings—pronounced "ESS-B-U-G-S," are droplets of liquid crystal that are applied to a polymer that's placed over a waveguide to make a grating "appear." When there's no voltage, the grating deflects a defined wavelength traveling in the waveguide. When voltage is applied, the grating disappears, and light travels straight through.

Ethernet

A standard originally devised for local area networks operating at 10 Mbits/s and utilizing CSMA/CD to regulate access to the network. Ethernet has since been extended to operate at higher speeds and adapted to better fit the needs of the public network.

external modulators

Components used to interrupt or permit the flow of laser light into the fiber.

Fabry-Perot laser

A laser in which the lasing cavity is surrounded on either end by a semireflective material. Once population inversion is reached, the light travels through this material, emitting light.

FDM

Frequency-division multiplexing—a way of combining multiple analog signals onto a single wire by sending each at a different carrier frequency.

FEC

Forward equivalence class—describing the flow of packets between two logical points that share certain common performance characteristics. These logical points might be between networks, devices, or even between processes in different devices.

femtometer

One quadrillionth of a meter.

fiber

Strands of glass used to carry optical signals.

fiber Bragg grating

A specially treated fiber with "stripes" of different refractive indices, reflecting a narrow range of selected wavelengths and transmitting others.

filters

Devices that attenuate particular frequencies or wavelengths but allow others to pass with relatively no change.

frame relay

A protocol used to build wide area networks that carry data as frames between destinations.

frequency

The number of wave oscillations per second. The higher the frequency, the shorter the wavelength.

FSAN

Full Service Access Network—consortium founded in 1995 by seven companies with the goal of creating a global specification for a high-speed, last-mile technology.

FSC interfaces

Fiber switch cable interfaces, which forward data based on the position of the data in physical space.

FSO

Free-space optics—the local loop technology that passes optical transmission through the air instead of fiber.

FTTB

Fiber to the building.

FTTC

Fiber to the curb.

FTTCab

Fiber to the cabinet—fiber pulled beyond the curb in a cabinet.

FTTH

Fiber to the home—fiber pulled to a residence.

FTTx

The generic term for all "Fiber To The 'x'" technologies, where x refers to home (h), building (b), curb (c), and cabinet (cab).

generalized switch

Type of switch that enables connections between one input port and many output ports or many input ports and one output port.

GI fiber

Graded index fiber—type of fiber that gets a significantly longer reach than step-index multimode fiber by gradually increasing the RI, reaching a high point in the middle of the fiber and then gradually decreasing toward the perimeter of the cable.

GMPLS

Generalized multiprotocol label switching—extending MPLS functionality to include non-IP elements such as crossconnects, wavelength routers, or optical add-drop multiplexers.

God-Box

A metro core device that combines large-range functions such as optical switching, ATM, and/or frame relay switching, IP routing, add-drop multiplexing, and DWDM.

grant numbers

The numbers that determine when the respective nodes on the PON can access the network.

grooming

The process of intelligently combining incoming data streams based on destination or some other criteria.

headend
The device on the end of the cable TV network that demodulates a cable TV signal.

hertz
A measure of a wave's frequency in cycles per second.

in-line amplifiers
Amplifiers that sit every 80 to 100 km along an optical fiber link, to make up for signal attenuation.

interference filters
Filters used in telecommunications for isolating frequencies between 1310 and 1550 nm.

interferometers
Components that employ the interference of light waves to measure the accuracy of optical surfaces.

IPX
Internetwork packet exchange—original network layer protocol used by Novell's NetWare network operating system.

isolator
A component that enables light to pass through but prevents it from traveling in the reverse direction.

ITU grid
International Telecommunications Union grid—standards for WDM channel spacing.

IXC
Interexchange carriers—pronounced "EYE-EX-SEES," that were the original long-distance carriers formed after the AT&T breakup.

jitter
Changes in delay between signals.

kilo
One thousand.

L2SC interfaces
Layer-2 switch capable interfaces—these recognize frame or cell boundaries and can forward data based on the content of the packet header.

lambda
The Greek symbol that's used to refer to wavelength.

laser
Light amplification by the stimulated emission of radiation—device typically used for transmitting light where distance or precision is required. Lasers work through the principle of stimulated emission to achieve highly precise, coherent light beams.

L-band
Long band—refers to the spectral range of wavelengths from 1565 to 1625 nm.

LDCs
Linear divider-combiners—special generalized switches that enable carriers to divide up input power among the output ports for better attenuation characteristics.

LDP
Label distribution protocol—used to distribute MPLS labels to enable LSPs to be established. Two types of LDPs are available—the resource reservation protocol (RSVP) and the constraint-based routing LDP (CR-LDP).

LED
Light-emitting diode—a junction comprised of a P-doped and an N-doped semiconductor. When a voltage is passed across the junction, energy is released in the form of light.

LER
Label edge router—the router that initiates the LSP in an MPLS network.

line

Within SONET, one of the individual circuits needed to compose a path. Each line is composed of multiple paths.

line filters

Interference filters that reflect or transmit one or two wavelengths.

liquid crystal switches

Switches that direct light through the use of liquid crystals. When a voltage is applied to a liquid crystal, the molecules shift position, changing certain properties such as their RI. The ability to change molecular alignment and RI means liquid crystals can be used in some interesting ways when it comes to switching. Exactly how they are used varies between implementations.

LMDS

Local multipoint distribution system—a licensed, fixed wireless technology running at 27.5 and 31.5 GHz. Offers higher speeds but shorter distances than MMDS.

long-distance network

The network connecting metropolitan networks.

longitudinal waves

Electromagnetic waves whose components oscillate or vibrate in parallel to the direction of a wave.

longpass filters

Filters that allow light having a wavelength greater than a certain value to pass.

LSC interfaces

Lambda switch capable interfaces—these forward data based on the wavelength on which it is received.

LSP

Label switched path—a provisioned flow of MPLS packets between two routers. LSPs are roughly analogous to circuits within ATM or frame relay.

LSR

Label switched router—one of the MPLS routers that sits between the LERs, enabling LSPs to be established.

Manchester encoding

An encoding scheme that represent ones and zeros through transitions in the middle of a bit.

Mbits/s

Millions of bits per second.

mega

One million.

MEM

Microelectromechanical—a device comprised of tiny moving parts. Within optics, MEMs are used to build all-optical switches with tiny mirrors that reflect signals between ports.

metropolitan network

A network spanning a town, city, or some other geographically confined area. The metropolitan network consists of access networks (the metro access networks) that feed into a central network (the metro core network).

microbends

Tiny bends in the fiber—often one cause of diffuse reflection.

micrometer

One millionth of a meter. Also called a micron.

millimeter

One thousandth of a meter.

MMDS

Multipoint multichannel distribution system—a licensed fixed wireless specification that operates between 2.1 and 2.7 GHz. Offers lower speeds but better range than LMDS.

modal dispersion

A form of dispersion that results from differences in the time the waves composing a light pulse take to travel across different modes.

mode coupling

Jumping of power between modes.

MPLS

Multiprotocol label switching—defines the next generation in routing, where networking decisions are based on short labels embedded in the packet instead of the network layer address.

multicast traffic

Traffic sent by one node to a defined number of receivers.

multimode

The presence of multiple light paths.

multimode fiber

A type of fiber cabling with a relatively large core (50 or 62.5 microns), providing multiple paths through which the waves that comprise a light pulse can travel.

multiplexer

A device that combines multiple signals into a single output.

NA

Numerical aperture—a measure of the size of the angle at which light can be injected into a multimode fiber and continue to propagate down that fiber.

nanometer

One billionth of a meter.

N-doped

Negatively charged semiconductor.

NDSF

Non-dispersion-shifted fiber—fiber having a stepped index core to increase transmission distances. Also called standard single-mode fiber.

neutral density filters

Filters that reduce transmission evenly across a portion of the spectrum.

NNI

Network-to-network interface—a piece of software that enables provider equipment to learn the full topology of the provider's network. Within OTN there are external NNIs (ENNIs) for connecting between a provider's domains and internal NNIs (INNIs) for connecting within a domain.

normal

An imaginary perpendicular line drawn at the point of intersection between an electromagnetic wave and the object it strikes.

NZDSF

Non-zero dispersion shifted fiber—introduces a nominal amount of dispersion to enable the fiber to work with DWDM systems and with the best amplifiers, EDFAs. *See* DSF and ZDSF.

OADM

See ADM.

OAN

Optical access network—passive optical network.

O-band

Original band—refers to the spectral range of wavelengths from 1260 to 1360 nm.

OC

Optical carrier—the optical equivalent of STS-3 and higher.

ODN

Optical distribution network—one branch within a passive optical network.

ODU

Optical channel data unit—an information structure defined in the OTN set of standards for transporting traffic across an optical channel. ODUs consist of the actual information payload, the Optical channel Payload Unit (OPU), and related overhead. The ODU is written as OTUk where, like the OTM, k can be either 1 (2.5 Gbits/s), 2 (10 Gbits/s) and 3 (40 Gbits/s).

OEO switches

Optical-electrical-optical switches—these convert optical signals into electrical form before switching them between ports. Also called opaque switches.

OLT

Optical line terminal—a special kind of switch used in passive optical networks that sits at the central office controlling network access and managing the passive network.

OMSs

Optical multiplex sections—within OTN, these are the WDM portions that underpin optical channels.

ONT

Optical network termination—device in a PON that sits in customer premises terminating the PON connection.

ONU

Optical network unit—device in a PON that converts between the PON signal and typically some DSL-based technology.

OOO switches

Optical-optical-optical switches—these direct optical signals between ports without first converting them into electrical signals. Also called all-optical switches or transparent switches.

opaque switches

See OEO switches.

optical crossconnect

A device that switches very large optical signals between ports.

optomechanical switches

Switches that connect two ports by mechanically moving a fiber.

OSI

Open systems interconnection—a model providing a generic representation of how any network should function.

OSPF

Open shortest path first—a popular routing protocol that finds the shortest path through an IP network.

OSPF-TE

Open shortest path first for traffic engineering—routing protocol used with MPLS to calculate the shortest path between two points based on traffic engineering parameters assigned to the links by the network designer. OSPF-TE is used for calculating routes within an AS.

OTM

Optical transport module—the basic increment used in the OTN hierarchy. OTMs are written with two numbers attached to them as OTM-n.[r]m. The "n" in this case represents the the maximum number of wavelengths that can be supported at the lowest bit rate on the wavelength. The "m" represents the bit rate or set of bit rates supported at the interface. The bit rates are indicated by "k" and can be either 1 (2.5 Gbits/s), 2 (10 Gbits/s), and 3 (40 Gbits/s). Bit rate combinations are also supported so six values are possible: 1, 2, 3, 12, 123, and 23. The "r" is optional (hence the brackets) and indicates reduced functionality OTMs.

OTN

Optical transport network—an emerging set of specifications from the ITU that defines a high-speed, switched architecture, widely expected to be SONET's successor for environments requiring large amounts of capacity. The interface for the OTN is defined in the ITU-T standard G.709 and at one time erroneously referred to as a "digital wrapper." The digital wrapper is more accurately described by the terms OTU and ODU.

OTS

Optical transmission section—the very bottom of the OTN hierarchy, describing the transmissions over individual fiber spans.

OTU

Optical transmission unit—transports the ODU over one or more optical channel connections. The OTU consists of the ODU and some overhead for managing an optical channel connection as well as the FEC for catching errors. The OTU is written as OTUk where, like the OTM, k can be either 1 (2.5 Gbits/s), 2 (10 Gbits/s), and 3 (40 Gbits/s).

overlay model

A public network architecture using various interfaces so that client equipment, equipment within the provider network, and equipment within a different domain in the provider's network can have access to different amounts of network information.

path

Within SONET, the connection between the two nodes that's comprised of a series of lines.

payload

The amount of data carried in a frame or packet.

PDFA

Prasedymium-doped fiber amplifier—it dopes a fiber with the element prasedymium and shows promise for amplifying signals at 1300 nm.

P-doped

Positively charged semiconductor.

peer-to-peer model

A public network architecture where nodes share the same amount of information about the network.

period

The number of times a cycle crosses a particular point in space.

permutation switches

Switches that enable only point-to-point links between different ports. One-to-many connections are not possible.

peta

One quadrillion.

phase

Relationship of the crests and troughs of two waves. Two waves that are in phase arrive at their crests and troughs at the same time.

photon

A particle of light.

photonic crossconnect
See Photonic switch.

photonic switch
Switch that divides transmission from a port into its wavelength components and then makes separate switching decisions for each wavelength. Also called a wavelength router or photonic crossconnect.

picometer
One trillionth of a meter.

PLOAM
Physical layer operations and maintenance—the cells within the PON technology that carry grant numbers.

polarization
In light waves, the direction in which the electric field vibrates. Linearly polarized light occurs when the electric field vibrates in the same direction all the time. Elliptically or circularly polarized light occurs when the plane that the electrical field vibrates within rotates around the wave's axis.

polarization fiber
A type of fiber that alters the RI to compensate for a dispersion problem called polarization mode dispersion (PMD).

PON
Passive optical network—last-mile network that employs no powered or active electronics to deliver the signal the last mile.

population inversion
A point in time with a laser where there are more atoms in an excited state than in the ground state, causing the release of laser light.

postamplifiers
Amplifiers located directly after a transmitter that increase the strength of a signal before transmission.

preamplifiers
Amplifiers that sit just before a receiver and magnify the signal to a power level within the receiver's sensitivity range.

priority queuing
A queuing scheme that places packets of different priorities in different queues, giving the highest-priority queue preferred access to the network.

protocols
A set of rules that guide communication between devices.

PSC interface
Packet switch capable interface—an interface that recognizes packet boundaries and can forward data based on the content of the packet header.

PVCs
See VCs.

QoS scheme
The algorithm or architecture used for providing bandwidth of different qualities to different applications or users.

Raman amplifiers
Amplifiers that use the Raman effect to boost signals at 1300, 1400, and 1500 nm. *See* Raman effect.

Raman effect
A change in frequency and wavelength observed when light is scattered in a transparent material. Named after the Indian physicist Sir Chandrasekhara Venkata Raman.

Raman scattering
A form of scattering whereby light waves absorb additional energy from atoms, scattering the light and changing the light's wavelength. *See* Raman effect.

Raman spectrum

A line of colors produced from the longer and shorter wavelengths as a result of the Raman effect. *See* Raman effect.

RBOC

Regional Bell Operating Companies—the seven local providers formed after the AT&T breakup.

rearrangeably nonblocking switches

Switches that have to move existing connections in the switching matrix to accommodate a new connection.

reflection

The bouncing of the light wave off a particular object.

refraction

The bending of light due to changes in the wave's speed as it passes between substances of different reflective indicies.

regenerator

A device that receives a signal, removes noise and distortion, and then retransmits the signal.

repeater

A device that receives a signal, converts it into electronic form, and then retransmits the signal.

RI

Refractive index—the ratio of the speed of light in a vacuum to the speed of light in a material.

router

A device that directs packets to a particular port based on a Layer-3 address, also called the network address.

routing protocols

Networking software used by routers to pass shared information about routing topology with the goal of finding the optimum path for moving packets through a network.

RPR

Resilient packet ring—a metro core technology being developed by the IEEE 802.17 working group. RPR aims to provide the low cost and efficiencies of Ethernet with the predictability, resilience, and support for ring topologies of SONET.

S-band

Short band—the spectral range of wavelengths from 1460 to 1530 nm.

scattering

A phenomenon whereby light is lost due to the scattering of atoms in different directions.

scrambled

The lightweight encryption algorithm used in PONs. The specification calls for a 24-bit encryption key.

SDH

Synchronous data hierarchy—the European equivalent of SONET.

section

Within SONET, sections are the physical line portions between amplifiers and regenerators.

semiconductor

Materials having conductivities lower than those of metals but higher than those of insulators.

Shannon's theorem

A theory that says the capacity of a channel increases inversely with the amount of noise in the channel.

shortpass filters

Filters that allow light with a wavelength less than a certain value to pass.

sockets

A high-layer interface enabling applications to address one another from across the network.

SONET

Synchronous optical network—a widespread standard among carriers for fiber optic transmission.

SONET payload

The portion of the SONET frame where data is carried. Within the payload is the SPE.

source address

The address of a station sending a frame or packet.

spatial reuse technology

The ability to use the same wavelengths between two different sets of nodes for carrying different transmissions.

SPE

Synchronous payload envelope—within a SONET frame, the location where the actual data is contained. Due to synchronization issues, VCs span successive SONET payloads.

specular reflection

The event where parallel light rays strike a surface and reflect off as parallel rays.

spontaneous emission

The release of photons when electrons fall to a lower energy level.

SRP

Spatial reuse protocol—Cisco technology eventually proposed as a suggested RPR standard.

step index multimode fiber

A type of fiber that keeps the same RI across the core's diameter.

stimulated emission

The process of encouraging the build-up of photons by preventing electrons from falling to their lower energy level.

strict-sense nonblocking switches

Switches that avoid rerouting connections altogether, though at the expense of additional hardware complexity.

STS

Synchronous transport signal—the fundamental signal in SONET. It operates at a rate of about 51 Mbits/s and has a payload capacity of 44.736 Mbits/s.

SVCs

See VCs.

switch

A device that directs optical or electrical signals from one path to another, usually using minimal information from the data stream. Switches operate at different layers within the network. Optical or electrical switches move light or electricity between ports with no insight into the data stream. Phone switches forward information based on the phone number dialed. Ethernet switches just use information within the Ethernet header to make their switching decision. ATM switches do the same, based on information contained in the ATM header.

TCP/IP

Transmission control protocol/internet protocol—a layered architecture predating the OSI model and today underlying the Internet and much of corporate data traffic.

TDM

Time-division multiplexing—a way of sequentially taking a bit or byte of data from multiple data streams and combining them to form a single data stream.

TDM interface

Time-division-multiplex capable interface—forwards data based on the data's time slot in a repeating cycle.

thermal-optic switches

Switches that change the velocity of light through a waveguide by changing the temperature of the material and thereby directing the light signal between ports.

total internal reflection

See Critical angle.

transparent switches

See OOO switches.

transverse waves

Electromagnetic waves in which components oscillate perpendicular to the motion of the wave.

U-band

Ultralong band—the spectral range of wavelengths from 1625 to 1675 nm.

UNI

User network interface—software that hides the complexity of the provider's network from those outside the network. Clients use the UNI to request services from the provider's network but can't peer inside the network to learn proprietary information.

VCI

Virtual channel identifier—the field within the ATM cell that specifies the channel or circuit to which the cell belongs.

VCs

Virtual circuits—flows between two or more nodes in an ATM network that are either temporary [switched virtual circuits (SVCs)] or permanent [permanent virtual circuits (PVCs)].

VCSELs

Vertical cavity semiconductor lasers—lasers that emit light from their tops, making them easier to manufacture than edge emitters.

VLANs

A way of associating computers defining workgroups that are logically distinct from one another, although connected over a common physical wire.

VPI

Virtual path identifier—the field within the ATM cell that specifies the path to which the cell belongs.

VPNs

Virtual private networks—service where by nodes or sites are connected securely together over a common network. VPNs typically consists of encrypting the traffic and authenticating the participants in the group.

VTs

Virtual tributaries—SONET channels spanning 1.544 Mbits/s (VT-1.5) to 6.312 Mbits/s (VT-6). VTs are aggregated together to form an STS-N signal. They are also called lower-order signals.

WAN PHY

The portion of the 10 Gbits/s Ethernet specification that describes how to pack 10 Gbits/s Ethernet packets within a SONET frame.

waveguide

A structure that channels or guides an electromagnetic wave. Fiber is an optical waveguide.

wavelength

The distance between the successive wave peaks.

wavelength routers

See Photonic switches.

WDM

Wave-division multiplexing—a way of combining multiple signals onto a single fiber by transmitting them at different wavelengths through that fiber.

weighted fair queuing

A queuing algorithm that ensures predictable service among different traffic classes.

wide-sense nonblocking switches

Switches that avoid rearranging active connections, assuming that the right rules for routing new connections are used.

WWDM

Wide wavelength-division multiplexing—multiplexing where the channel spacing is greater than 200 GHz.

XAUI

X (as in the Roman numeral for 10) attachment unit interface—a high-speed bus used by 10 Gbits/s Ethernet to simplify board layout.

XGMII

A 32-bit data path that enables existing Ethernet chips to be used with 10 Gbits/s Ethernet's new XAUI high-speed bus.

yotta

One septillion.

ZDSF

Zero dispersion-shifted fiber—fiber that alters the RI in such a way as to eliminate dispersion from the signal. *See* DSF and NZDSF.

Bibliography

Allen, Doug, *Passive Optical Networking Brings DSL to the Masses*, Network Magazine, http://www.networkmagazine.com/article/NMG20001103S0007, 2000.

Allen, Doug, *The Second Coming of Free Space Optics*, Network Magazine, http://www.network-magazine.com/article/NMG20010226S0007, 2001.

Ashwood-Smith, Peter; Awduche, Daniel; Banerjee, Ayan; Basak, Debashis; Berger, Lou; Bernstein, Greg; Drake, John; Fan, Yanhe; Fedyk, Don; Grammel, Gert; Kompella, Kireeti; Kullberg, Alan; Lang, Jonathan P.; Liaw, Fong; Nadeau, Thomas D.; Papadimitriou, Dimitri; Pendarakis, Dimitrios; Rajagopalan, Bala; Rekhter, Yakov; Saha, Debanjan; Sandick, Hal; Sharma, Vishal; Swallow, George; Tang, Z. Bo; Yu, John; and Zinin, Alex, edited by Mannie, Eric, *Internet-Draft: Generalized Multi-Protocol Label Switching (GMPLS) Architecture*, http://www.ietf.org/internet-drafts/draft-ietf-ccamp-gmpls-architecture-00.txt, 2001.

Ashwood-Smith, Peter; Banerjee, Ayan; Berger, Lou; Bernstein, Greg; Drake, John; Fan, Yanhe; Kompella, Kireeti; Mannie, Eric; Lang, Jonathan P.; Rajagopalan, Bala; Rekhter, Yakov; Saha, Debanjan; Sharma, Vishal; Swallow, George; and Tang, Z. Bo, *Internet-Draft: Generalized MPLS-Signaling Functional Description*, http://www.ietf.org/internet-drafts/draft-ietf-mpls-generalized-signaling-06.txt, 2001.

Awduche, Daniel O.; Chiu, Angela; Elwalid, Anwar; Widjaja, Indra; and Xiao, XiPeng, *Internet-Draft: Internet Traffic Engineering*, http://www.ietf.org/internet-drafts/draft-ietf-tewg-principles-01.txt, 2001.

Awduche, D; Malcolm, J.; Agogbua, J.; O'Dell, M.; and McManus, J., *Requirements for Traffic Engineering Over MPLS (RFC 2702)*, http://www.ietf.org/rfc/rfc2702.txt, 1999.

Chiu, Angela; Tkach, Robert; Luciani, James; Banerjee, Ayan; Drake, John; Blumenthal, Dan; Fredette, Andre; and Froberg, Nan, edited by Strand, John, *Internet-Draft: Impairments and Other Constraints On Optical Layer Routing*, http://www.ietf.org/internet-drafts/draft-ietf-ipo-impairments-00.txt, 2001.

Clavenna, Scott and Heywood, Peter, *Optical Taxonomy*, Light Reading, http://www.lightreading.com/document.asp?doc_id=3780, 2001.

Davie, Bruce and Rekhter, Yakov, *MPLS: Technology and Applications*, San Francisco: Morgan Kaufmann, 2000.

Dodd, Annabel Z., *The Essential Guide to Telecommunications, Third Edition*, Upper Saddle River, NJ: Prentice-Hall, Inc., 2002.

Dornan, Andy, *The Essential Guide to Wireless Communications Applications,* Upper Saddle River, NJ: Prentice-Hall, Inc., 2001.

Dornan, Andy, *Frozen Light*, Network Magazine,

Dutton, Harry, *Understanding Optical Communications*, Upper Saddle River, NJ: Prentice-Hall, Inc., 1999.

European Telecommunications Standards Institute, *System Description for DTM*, http://www.etsi.org/t_news/0105_span_dtm.htm, 2001.

Greenfield, David, *Fiber and Optical Networking*, Network Magazine, http://www.networkmagazine.com/article/NMG20010619S0003, 2001.

Greenfield, David, *The Optical Revolution*, Network Magazine, http://www.networkmagazine.com/article/NMG20000510S0011, 2000.

Greenfield, David, *Optical Standards: A Blueprint for the Future*, Network Magazine, http://www.networkmagazine.com/article/NMG20011004S0004, 2001.

Hecht, Jeff, *Understanding Fiber Optics, Fourth Edition,* Upper Saddle River, NJ: Prentice-Hall, Inc., 2002.

Hecht, Jeff, *Understanding Fiber Optics, Third Edition,* Upper Saddle River, NJ: Prentice-Hall, Inc., 1999.

Herrera, Albert; White, Russ; Jha, Pankaj K.; Sharma, Raj; Agrawal, Sanjay; Jogalekar, Prasad; Sastry, Arun; and Amer, Khaled, *Internet-Draft: A Framework for IP over RPR*, http://www.ietf.org/internet-drafts/draft-ietf-iporpr-framework-01.txt, 2001.

Heywood, Peter; Rigby, Pauline; and Clavenna, Scott, *Optical Switching Fabric*, Light Reading, http://www.lightreading.com/document.asp?doc_id=2254, 2000.

Institute of Electrical and Electronics Engineers Standards for Local and Metropolitan Area Networks, *Virtual Bridged Local Area Networks (802.1Q)*, http://standards.ieee.org/reading/ieee/std/lanman/802.1Q-1998.pdf, 1999.

IUN/FYDE Introductory Physics Notes, http://theory.uwinnipeg.ca/physics/index.html, 1996.

Jander, Mary, *PONs: Passive Aggression*, Light Reading, http://www.lightreading.com/document.asp?doc_id=486, 2000.

Langa, Fred, *From QuBits to the Ultimate PC*, Byte.com, http://www.byte.com/documents/s=459/byt20000920s0001, 2000.

Nadeau, Thomas D.; Chiu, Angela; Townsend, William; and Skalecki, Darek, *Internet-Draft: Extensions to RSVP-TE and CR-LDP for support of Diff-Serv-Aware MPLS Traffic Engineering*, http://www.ietf.org, 2001.

Network Magazine, *News and Analysis*, http://www.networkmagazine.com/article/NMG20010319S0007, 2001.

Physics 2000, http://www.colorado.edu/physics/2000/index.pl?Type=TOC, 2000.

Ramaswami, Rajiv and Sivarajan, Kumar, *Optical Networks: A Practical Perspective, Second Edition*, San Francisco: Morgan Kaufmann, 2001.

Saunders, Stephen, *Data Communications Gigabit Ethernet Handbook*, New York: McGraw-Hill, 1998.

Serway, Raymond A. and Beichner, Robert J., *Physics for Scientists and Engineers with Modern Physics, Fifth Edition*, Orlando, FL: International Thomson Publishing, 2000.

Stallings, William, *ISDN: An Introduction*, New York: Macmillan, Inc., 1989.

Stern, Thomas E. and Bala, Krishna, *Multiwavelength Optical Networks: A Layered Approach*, Upper Saddle River, NJ: Prentice-Hall, Inc, 1999.

Stored Program Optical Computer (SPOC), http://ece-www.colorado.edu/~harry/spoc/spoc.html, 1994.

T1XI A Technical Subcommittee of Standards Committee, *Carrier Optical Services Framework and Associated Requirements for UNI*, http://www.t1.org, 2000.

T1XI A Technical Subcommittee of Standards Committee, *Synchronous Optical Network (SONET) Sub STS-1 Interface Rates and Formats Specification (ANSI T1.105.07-1996)*, http://www.t1.org, 1996.

Techfest, "SONET/SDH Technical Summary," http://www.techfest.com, 1999.

Tektronix, *SONET Telecommunications Standard Primer*, http://www.tek.com/Measurement/App_Notes/SONET/welcome.html, 2001.

Telecommunication Standardization Sector of International Telecommunications Union, *Framework for Optical Transport Network Recommendations (G.871/Y.1301)*, http://www.itu.org, 2000.

Telecommunication Standardization Sector of International Telecommunications Union, *Interface for Optical Transport Network (G.709) Prepublished Recommendation*, http://www.itu.org, 2001.

Telecommunication Standardization Sector of International Telecommunications Union, *Architecture for Optical Transport Network Recommendations (G.872)*, http://www.itu.org, 1999.

Telecommunication Standardization Sector of International Telecommunications Union, *Broadband Optical Access Systems Based on Passive Optical Networks (PONS) (G.983.1)*, http://www.itu.org, 1998.

Telecommunication Standardization Sector of International Telecommunications Union, *Optical Interfaces for Multichannel Systems with Optical Amplifiers (G.692)*, http://www.itu.org, 1998.

The Light Guide, http://www.vislab.usyd.edu.au/photonics/index.html, 1999.

Thinkquest, http://library.thinkquest.org/C005705/English/Light/light1.htm, 2001.

Walker, Jearl, *Light*, Discovery Channel School, original content provided by World Book Online, http://www.discoveryschool.com/homeworkhelp/worldbook/atozscience/l/32326.html, 2001.

Index